D1498023

DEMCO

Where Flows
the
Ganges

John Samuel Whipple

Where Flows the Ganges

The Story of

John Samuel Whipple

Missionary

to

INDIA

by

Juanita Owen

Lakeland Color Press
Brainerd, MN 56401

Where Flows the Ganges

Library of Congress Catalogue
Card Number 78-61019

Printed in The United States of America

To
Those Young People of Every Land
Who Are Now on the Threshold
of Their Life Vocation
This Book
Is Affectionately Inscribed

ACKNOWLEDGMENTS

Special thanks are due my sister, Bernice Owen Fordham, for reviving and rescuing this manuscript from oblivion. Also to Dorothy Vellenga my deepest appreciation for reading the proofs and correcting errors.

All quotations from the Bible are from the King James Version. A sincere effort has been made to credit the authorship of quotations and bits of poetry and, where I have been unsuccessful in tracing the authors, forgiveness is begged.

Thanks to Muriel Whipple Haddon, John Chauncey Whipple, and Marjorie Whipple Johnson for contributing family pictures. All other photographs with the exception of the picture of Kanchenjunga and the Taj Mahal are by the author as are the pen and ink drawings which were for the most part sketched on the spot.

J.O.

ILLUSTRATIONS

9

PEN AND INK SKETCHES

TABLE OF CONTENTS

FOREWORD

On the evening of April 26, 1930, as I returned from an Indian village, a telegram was handed to me telling of Mr. Whipple's illness up in the Himalayas and, just a week later, I stood by his open grave, where in the providence of God no other friend or relative was permitted to be, wondering God's purpose in it all. Mr. Whipple's life had meant a great deal to me and right by his graveside a great longing swept over me to pass on to others a little of the inspiration I had received from his godly life.

During the summer that followed, this story, as it now stands, began to take shape in my mind. Night after night, during those hot months when sleep was driven from us, I drew from Mrs. Whipple the story of those early days which I pass on to you. It was my privilege to know Mr. Whipple personally throughout the later years of his life; so much of what is written of those years is from personal observation.

Thanks are due to those of his co-workers on the field who have kindly given information and much valued criticism, as well as working on the manuscript and preparing it for the press.

One verse from the Bible has been ringing in my ears and has urged me on when time, inability, and circumstances seemed to forbid it: "If by any means I may provoke to emulation them which are my flesh, and might save some of them." May God use this story to perpetuate the influence of Mr. Whipple's life and kindle a desire in other young people to give their lives in the spread of the Gospel as he did.

J.O.

Darjeeling, India

Chapter I

CHILDHOOD DAYS

"A boy's will is the wind's will,
And the thoughts of youth are long, long thoughts."

—Henry W. Longfellow

Blessings on thee, little man,
Barefoot boy, with cheeks of tan!
With thy turned-up pantaloons,
And thy merry whistled tunes;
With thy red lips; redder still
Kissed by strawberries on the hill;
With the sunshine on thy face,
Through thy torn brim's jaunty grace,
From my heart I give thee joy, —
I was once a barefoot boy.

—John Greenleaf Whittier

The Whipple Farm in Connecticut

Chapter I

CHILDHOOD DAYS

IT was one of those cold, wet evenings in early spring. The long winter's snow had melted leaving only slush and mud in each footpath and highway and, to add to the dismal outlook, a chill April rain pattered against the window pane in a sort of iambic rhythm. Picking up the evening paper and his book of Whittier's poems, John drew his chair up to the fire and almost unconsciously began to poke the coals.

Father was tired from his day's labors on the farm and had already gone to bed. The supper dishes being finished, Mother brought her large market basket filled to its capacity with rosy apples from the well-stocked cellar and, seating herself in her favorite rocking chair by the fireside, silently began paring the pile of apples before her.

John Whipple was the stay-at-home type and in the long winter evenings when his brothers were off to the neighbors' farm he would while away the evening reading or chatting with Mother around the kitchen fireplace.

Again John picked up his book—he had always loved to read—but somehow it held no interest for him tonight, so he let it drop listlessly into his lap, starting up as he did so to stir the fire once more with the big iron poker. Then he sat down only to jump up again with a start and pace to and from the window where the rain still beat its ceaseless dirge against the steamy panes.

It was evident that something was troubling John and when he finally threw himself once more into his accustomed chair by the fire Mother ventured a query: "You're not yourself tonight, John. Tell me what happened."

"Nothing, Mother. Just don't care to read tonight. Guess it's the weather." But Mother was not quite sure that it was "nothing" that was troubling him and making that anxious, faraway look in his eyes.

John's parents were old New England residents, and it was in the village of Ledyard that he was born on the nineteenth day of July, 1884. John's father, James Eldon Whipple, was one of a long line of men of letters and of distinction in the history of New England. A paternal uncle was a general at Bunker Hill who received several medals for bravery, and another ancestor, William Whipple, was one of the signatories to the Declaration of Independence.

James Whipple had chosen one of the few occupations open to young men of his day—pedagogy—of the old-fashioned type. He was both lawgiver and justice of the peace in his one-room schoolhouse where he ruled firmly but kindly with the aid of the proverbial "hickory stick," which Washington Irving declared was absolutely essential to that "sagacious pedagogue who would urge the tardy loiterers along the flowery path of knowledge." James Whipple won for himself a reputation for discipline in the surrounding countryside when he dealt with a too-active prankster that had defaced a just-last-year's spelling book with a jackknife.

Not only could he read and cipher but it was soon known around the village that he was acquainted with the classics as well and knew history and had read the Bible through from cover to cover, and he could quote verbatim from the poets. Poetry was known to be his favorite pastime and many long winter evenings he would spend with Whittier, Emerson, Tennyson, or Milton while he was "boardin' round."

It began to be whispered at the village husking parties and quilting bees that James Whipple had a particular fondness for a certain young lady pupil of his. The months sped by and it happened just as many of the good Quakertown housewives said it would happen—James Whipple married Jeannette Williams who still had a couple of years left of her teens. She also, coincidentally, was a descendant of a signer of the Declaration of Independence, having the same Christian name, William Williams. Jeannette Whipple proved in every way suited to be the wife of the village schoolmaster. She appreciated his bent for learning and aspired with him to make their home a place of refinement and culture. Early it was decided that, should they be blessed with sons and daughters, each alternate child should be given the name of a poet and each alternate one a Bible name.

The Whipple home was situated on a wild, rocky craig which was known in all the surrounding countryside as Lantern Hill; the name derived from the fact that, years ago, when America was a land of the Red Man, the Indians used Lantern Hill for a lookout

17

post. Here in times of danger, messages were sent to the surrounding tribes by means of a lantern hoisted on the top of this hill which could be seen for many miles; so I have been told by the residents of those parts—but I have also heard the explanation that near the summit there is a quarry of fine white marble and the bright light of the sun on this rock is reflected for miles around, hence its appropriate name. Whatever the source, the young people of the surrounding country loved this hillock and it was a favorite picnic ground for all in those early days.

When John was still very small his family moved to Gallop Hill and his early education was received at the little Gallop Hill country school where, day after day, he trudged to school with a knotted, four-cornered handkerchief on his head, humming or whistling to the birds as he passed by. After school hours his time was spent in helping out on the farm. In the evening when the cows had been milked, the horses fed, the chickens locked up, and everything arranged for the night, John would hie him to his books in his cheery place by the kitchen fireside.

His parents were not religious. They lived moral, honest lives but never taught their children to attend church, to pray, or to observe the Sabbath. It was a great delight to John after being confined all week in the schoolroom to roam out on Sunday to a nearby creek or river and while away the afternoon fishing or skating. When John was still quite young the Whipple family moved into Quakertown—a beautiful little village tucked away among the rolling hills of old Connecticut —and it was there that he spent the remainder of his boyhood days.

The Crouch family, too, were old one-time residents of Quakertown but of recent years the father's business had taken them to Center Groton three or four miles away. Each Sunday morning the horses were harnessed to the quaint double-seated carriage and the Crouch family including their daughter Jessie were off to the Quakertown Chapel for the Sunday School and morning meeting.

Two of her cousins were Jessie's almost constant companions and many merry times they had together. She was a regular attendant at the Sunday School and nearly every Sunday found her seated along with the other girls and boys of the neighborhood to receive instruction from the Word of God.

One Sunday morning as she sat in her accustomed place she noticed a new face. The teacher had arranged her scholars in two long rows facing each other, the boys on one long bench and the little girls on the other. Just opposite where she was sitting there was a new scholar and when Jessie saw his big round face and closely shaven hair she thought she had never before seen anyone so amusing. But there was something about those large blue eyes that she could not forget though she did not see him again for many months. Nor did the fat-faced, bald-headed little boy of twelve ever forget the red-haired girl with the pretty blue frock who had sat opposite him.

A few years passed and the Crouch family moved back into the Quakertown district and—as Providence would have it—into the house just over the way from the Whipple home which was clearly visible through the trees and sumac bushes that edged the fields and pasture. Then it was that John often found occasions to visit the Crouch farm and Jessie was quick to perceive that his mind was not so wholly occupied with poultry, eggs and farm stuff as he feigned. A long friendship was the result. They would often stroll together in the open fields or gather violets in the woods nearby, but most favorite of all was the lane that led down to Punch Bowl.

Springtime has always had a lure all its own and calls bewitchingly to youth. In New England the spell is enhanced, no doubt, by the freedom from the long, severe winter, and the month of May seems to be the acme of all her charm and gaiety.

In those days May parties were in vogue and that particular year one had been planned for nearly every night of the month. Though it meant being out until midnight, Jessie never failed to make one of the jolly party. A May basket would be filled with sweetmeats or flowers and one of the party would hang it on a friend or neighbor's door while the rest of the group would hide close by to watch the fun. After hanging the basket and rapping loudly he would make off lest those in the house make chase, catch him and find him out. There usually followed a treat of cake, or a handout of sweets and candy.

Thus many springtimes with all their fun and merriment had come to the beautiful little village of Quakertown, and the spring of 1901 seemed to give promise of an added amount of mirth and good times. At the end of May Jessie would complete her seventeenth year and, as if the years before had lacked aught of being all that happy girlhood years should be, she crammed into that one month enough parties to more than fill up any deficient quota.

But all these enjoyments could not bring a sense of peace to Jessie's heart. She longed for something—she hardly knew what—to satisfy her inmost soul.

About that time a preacher came into the neighborhood and announced meetings in the little church: REVIVAL MEETINGS—the sign read. That was something new, something different from the round of parties and social life and she decided to attend.

There was something about the earnestness of that preacher, something in the shine on his face that impressed her. She knew he was a genuine Christian and then too, she knew she was not. She had thought many times of her sins and they lay like a great burden upon her heart. "If I were to die now," she had often thought to herself, "would I be ready?" Something told her she would not be and the fear of dying made her tremble though not for all the world would she have admitted it to her friends and acquaintances.

One evening after the meeting someone spoke to her asking her if she would like to give her heart to Christ and become a *real* Christian. Perhaps it was from fear of her friends who were sitting close by or perhaps it was the fear of what it might cost later on; whatever the cause, Jessie answered "No." The words were scarcely spoken before she realized that she had not merely said "No" to the preacher but to the unseen Christ Himself and the thought nearly crushed her. All the way home she was thinking of what she had done. When she knelt down to pray that night she promised

God that if He would let her live until she had another opportunity she would give her heart to Him.

Next morning found her at her bedside praying earnestly that God would forgive her sins and make her His child. She surrendered herself wholeheartedly to Christ to follow Him and let Him direct her life, and the heavy burden was gone. Oh, the joy that filled her soul! She knew that her sins were forgiven and Christ had come into her heart. She was happy now. No longer did she care for the old pastimes and amusements; instead she loved to pray and nothing gave her greater pleasure than attending the revival meetings in the little Quakertown church.

His father being a farmer and always having lived on a farm, John early entertained ambitions of one day being a prosperous farmer himself. Often in his mind's eye would float pictures of rich farm lands, well-kept horses and large barns; and there was always featured in the scene a little white cottage with green shutters and pretty, neat curtains in the windows. Many, many times in his imagination he built and re-built that house; so often had he pictured all this in his mind that, as he told us afterwards, it became as real to him as life itself.

About this time John had a friend of whom he thought a great deal who was very spiritually minded. The two were often together, sometimes wandering into the woods for long walks, and many times in their conversation together Walter would talk of the future, of death and the hereafter. To John these subjects were dull and uninteresting. They cast a gloom over him and he preferred to think on brighter things. Walter took life too seriously, he thought. These were topics suited to hermits and philosophers—let John have his carefree farm life in the beautiful out-of-doors. Why should he trouble his mind brooding over such dismal, foreboding thoughts?

John too had attended the revival meetings held in the little church in Quakertown. Many of his friends and acquaintances had been convicted of their sins and had found God's forgiveness, among them his two brothers. John saw the change in their lives and he secretly longed that he too might find inner peace and happiness but what about those old ambitions? He had carefully made his plans for his life and those plans were dear to him. Was it possible that God was asking him to give up these long cherished hopes just now on the eve of their fulfillment? That was too great a demand. Even the earnest persuasion of his bosom friend did not move him, for his heart was set on that one thing—being a prosperous farmer.

One of their neighbors, a very successful farmer had been John's ideal. He had watched him thrive year after year and admired him greatly as he saw him now in the height of his prosperity. Very suddenly, almost without warning, this farmer died and was called to give his account before God. This deeply affected John and within he heard a voice say, "You will be just like that man. After you achieve your heart's desire for a fine home and a prosperous business, you will one day be taken away and have to leave it all." What a struggle waged in his heart! John found himself deeply troubled and perplexed.

So, as he sat by the fireside that chill April evening, he was thinking long, long thoughts. In his mind he would picture the scene his imagination had painted so vividly and which through the years had grown so dear to him. How could he relinquish his ambitions now just when they were about to be realized and surrender everything to Christ? Then simultaneously with these thoughts he would recall the recent meetings in the church and those gentle strivings of the Spirit of God and the promise of peace to his troubled heart if he would but yield.

This then was the dilemma that caused his anxiety and that far-away, restless look in his eye. The fire died down. John spoke a hasty goodnight to his mother and went upstairs to bed. Not only that night but for many weary nights to follow he tossed on his pillow, these troubling thoughts running over and over in his mind giving him no rest or peace. Yet all the while the great Father above stood watching and anxiously waited to give him the pardon and peace that comes to those who surrender.

Chapter II

THE HAYLOFT

"Thus passed a few swift years, and they no longer
were children;
He was a valiant youth, and his face, like the face of
the morning,
Gladdened the earth with its light, and ripened thought
into action.
She was a woman now, with the heart and hopes of a
woman."

—Longfellow

"Nothing can ever be dull again,
When once we fling our windows open wide
And see the mighty world that lies outside
And whisper to ourselves this wondrous thing—
'We're wanted for the business of the King.' "

Chapter II

THE HAYLOFT

UST a year had passed since that preacher had come into the little village of Quakertown and in that year's time many changes had taken place. People, who previously only took thought for their own affairs, now were interested in helping others; young folks, whose lives had consisted in amusements and pleasure, now forgot all about those things in their new-found joy in Christ. They enjoyed the prayer meetings which were blessed times frequently lasting a whole night.

It was a prayer meeting like one of these that was announced at his brother's home and John decided to go, just a small gathering but the Spirit of God was there. Perhaps no one present guessed the mighty struggle going on in his heart nor of the victory about to be won. They went to prayer, John kneeling beside a little keg in one side of the room. His heart was hungry and longing for peace. After all, what would it profit him if he should gain his earthly desires and then forever have to pay the penalty for having lived a selfish life?

He resolved right there that from henceforth he would be a pilgrim and a stranger in this world—a humble follower of the lowly Jesus. Suddenly he sprang to his feet. "Glory, glory, glory!" he began to shout, for he knew immediately that God had accepted him and made him His child.

From that night he was a different person. He knew he had been "born again," his mother and brothers knew it, and even the neighbors living miles away soon found out that John Whipple was a changed man. And oh, how different everything was! All the dark clouds had passed and life abounded with new joys. He began to read the Bible and prayer was now the delight of his soul. How good it was to live all the day through without doing anything that brought a load upon his conscience, and at night to lie down with no haunting fears of death overtaking him unprepared.

One day, not long after John's conversion, he proposed a walk with Jessie down the lane towards Punch Bowl. It was springtime and the air was fragrant with the scent of woodland flowers. It seemed all nature was flaunting herself in her new array of colors and adding her enchantment to the already charming landscape of that old New England village. John was serious and together they talked of the recent awakening in the Quakertown community and of the change that had come into their lives. Jessie spoke resolutely of her decision to live her life henceforth for God and His glory.

The sun was slowly setting in the western sky and little silver stars were just beginning to show when they started back down the lane toward Jessie's home. To John that day was a red-letter day and one long to be remembered for at last he had obtained the desired promise from Jessie who pledged him her loyalty while life should last. To Jessie, too, that day carried a great significance, for it seemed the days of her girlhood were ended and she had stepped over the threshold into that broader, nobler life—the realm of womanhood.

God then began to talk to John about giving his time and talents to preaching the Gospel. He had received largely from the hand of God and many souls had never so much as heard the name of Jesus. Would he go and be Christ's messenger to other sin-sick hearts? The call of God was on him and he knew it was the call of God. He knew, too, that it would involve leaving home and parents and everything he held dear and there was something within that rebelled at the thought of it.

Why must he go and serve in other spheres while so many around him were permitted to remain at home and serve their Master? But he did not then dream of the wide field of usefulness into which God was trying to lead him nor did he realize the rich recompense that accompanies faithful toil for the Master. He saw only the cross and felt that it was too great to bear. Satan again brought to his mind the picture of a comfortable home and farm and marrying the girl he had loved all these years but who now seemed so hopelessly far away, for Jessie had already obeyed the call and was now in the Bible School and Missionary Training Home in Wisconsin more than a thousand miles away!

Listening to these suggestions from the enemy, he lost the joy he had found and all the peace he had recently known. Now God seemed far away and John fell into one sin after another. He soon found himself even deeper in sin than he had ever known before his

29

conversion. He felt alarmed at his condition and longed to again have peace with God. He endeavored to keep busy with his work on the farm and sought in that way to keep his mind occupied.

John had a beautiful black mare of which he was very proud. Getting up one morning he went out to the stable to look at his horse but in just a few moments, without any warning, the horse fell dead at his feet. This forcibly brought to his mind the uncertainty of life and the folly of trusting in earthly riches. What was there in life after all, except it be to live for eternal things that cannot pass away? If only Jessie had never made up her mind to go away and leave him. He might have derived some pleasure from her company but now there were a thousand tantalizing miles between.

Then one day there came a letter. It was in the old familiar handwriting, and John eagerly tore open the envelope, hoping for something to cheer him. There it was again—the old troublesome question staring him in the face. Jessie was urging him to surrender to God and obey His call as she had done, and the thought of it all only made John the more miserable.

About this time, in the winter of 1905, revival meetings were again held in a nearby city and John made up his mind to attend. While those meetings were in progress the Spirit again began to work upon his heart and he once more weighed the question in his mind. He knew it would mean forsaking his old plans, leaving his home and his parents whom he loved with all the affection of a dutiful son. He was fondly attached to his mother and as he thought of their approaching old age, it seemed cruel and heartless to

leave them and go so far away. After all, was it not his duty to provide for his parents in their later years? Then he remembered that he had read in his Bible "He that loveth father or mother more than Me is not worthy of Me," and he knew too, that the One who clothed the lilies and fed the ravens would also care for his parents in their declining years. All the while the call of God was ringing in his ears and he dared hesitate no longer to give up his small earthly comforts and joys that he might become the messenger of Christ to carry the light to other souls sitting in darkness. He determined that, cost what it may, he would do it for the sake of the One who had done so much for him. With that decision the Lord again came near and the things of God once more became the delight of his life.

He decided to enter the Bible Training School to prepare for the ministry, for now he knew definitely that God wanted him to preach the Gospel. The day finally came when he was to say farewell to the home of his boyhood days and the scene of so many youthful joys. It had become to him a world all his own and he knew little of the big outside world awaiting him.

He boarded the westbound express train and soon the beautiful hills of old New England were left far behind. The plains of the west looked so bare and gave him a feeling of loneliness almost insufferable. Even on the journey Satan assailed him and suggested that he get off the train and go back home.

While in the Bible School both Jessie and John felt that since God led them to surrender their lives to Him, that surrender must include every phase of their lives, lest in holding on to one of their own personal plans, the great plan of God be thwarted and their whole after lives be warped or blighted. They were both convinced that their engagement must be dropped, not to be renewed unless reintroduced by God Himself as a part of His plan for their lives. Henceforth they determined to live for only one thing—to carry out the plan of their Heavenly Father and labor for the salvation of others.

This is where John's battle began afresh. He had surrendered without first sitting down and counting the cost, so when it came to saying goodbye forever, he suddenly became aware of what an absolute surrender really meant.

Many were the discouraging times and struggles of that first year in the Bible School. At one time he became so discouraged that he ran away from the school and stayed a week or two out in the country with some farmers. The first night he spent under a haystack for it was too late to find friends or secure a position. As he lay out in the open under the starry heavens he somehow felt nearer to God than he had for a long time. "What a fool I am," he thought, "to try to run away from God." The truth of that scripture in the Psalms was very real to him that night; "Whither shall I go from thy Spirit or whither shall I flee from thy presence? If I ascend up into heaven, thou art there: if I make my bed in hell, behold, thou art there."

Just as the Spirit of God had followed him, Satan was also on his track. "You have made such a fool of yourself now, you cannot go back," he tantalizingly suggested. Two long weeks were spent working for a German farmer, but somehow farm life did not appeal to John as it had before he heard the call. "Fool or no fool, I'm going back," he determined. Prodigal-like, he retraced his steps and Sunday morning found him back in the Bible School seated along with the other students in the morning service.

But why should he have such a hard time? Others around him had victory and why should he not have it? Then John Whipple made up his mind that if there was any possible way he would find out the secret.

Seeking out a spot where he might be alone with his God he wandered down to the old horse-barn in the back of the school. It was large and roomy and, as it was now late, he was sure no one would enter. Climbing up to the hayloft he knelt down in the straw and began to pray. In his anxiety of heart he cried out to God for deliverance, and that very night God heard his cry.

Before long his voice was ringing in the loft and he knew that he had touched God. That battles would still come he was well aware but he knew he had a Friend who would help him through. From that day when God met him in the hayloft he never swerved from his course. That day marked the beginning of a steady purpose and all his energies were devoted to the spread of the Gospel. All selfish plans were forever forgotten and the record of his life from that time is the history of a life of disinterested service and devotion in the cause which now claimed all his ransomed powers.

Chapter III

FAR AWAY VOICES CALLING

"The Master's ringing cry is: 'Go ye' and the other cry from our brothers of the far-away lands is: 'You are a long time coming.' "

—Gordon

The Fountain Spring House.

And I will go. I may no longer doubt
To give up friends, and home, and idle hopes,
And every tender tie that binds my heart
To thee my country! Why should I regard
Earth's little store of borrowed sweets? I sure
Have had enough of bitter in my cup,
To show that never was it His design
Who placed me here, that I should live in ease
Or drink at pleasure's fountain.

—Rev. Nathan Brown, Assam.

Chapter III

FAR AWAY VOICES CALLING

T is interesting to trace the dealings of God in the lives of those who have given themselves to Him. How many times we see that the weak points in their characters become the strong ones. From that day in the hayloft Mr. Whipple's life was different. It marked the beginning of a steadfastness of purpose and an end to the vacillation which had characterized him until now. He had unreservedly placed his life and his future in the hands of the Master and from that time on his story is one of faithful and unrelenting service and devotion.

And think you such a life slave-like? Listen! He had come to know that should he gain in this world all that his heart could desire, in the end it would leave only an aching void. God was to plan his life far better than he could ever do and he had placed his all into the hands of the Great Potter to mold and fashion for His glory. From that moment God began to work out His perfect plan in John's life and the vessel grew in symmetry and in usefulness.

Mr. Whipple began to teach school and his thirty or forty bright little scholars soon learned to love him as the champion of their cause. He felt he had a responsibility greater than merely instilling knowledge into their young minds. He strove to instill those principles of uprightness and integrity that God had recently been implanting in his own heart. Mr. Whipple was making rapid progress in his spiritual life and friends and others at the Bible School were compelled to take note of it.

One day as he was going about his regular duties the superintendent met him and faced him with a question: Did he still care for Miss Crouch and would he like to renew their friendship? Of course he did! And his heart leaped for very joy at the thought of it. What matter that nearly four years had passed by since they were sweethearts back in old Connecticut—four years of trial and struggle, four years of almost total silence between them? Now those precious little missives often flew from one to the other and brought cheer and gladness with them like the birds of springtime.

Summer came and with it vacation. John spent the first six weeks of the summer at Rockford, Illinois, assisting in a series of evangelistic meetings. It was here he learned to wait upon God for his messages and to face an audience without fainting even though he said his "feet shook both ways." This was valuable training for the days that lay ahead when he would stand before much larger audiences not only in his native land but in distant lands as well.

Jessie and John had known all along that they were meant for each other and their tacit engagement only waited for God to reveal to them His will for their lives. So they prayed and waited.

Then one day there came a telegram calling John back to the school where he was to be married in just a few days. To John this was welcome news, indeed. Arriving at Waukesha late Saturday night he did not even get a glimpse of the one who was to be his bride, nor on Sunday, and the wedding had been planned for the day after! Strange vicissitudes, we would say, but a hand above was preparing him for far stranger, far more costly sacrifices on a wider battlefield.

In the parlor of the Bible School a group of friends, relatives and fellow-students were gathered that memorable day, July 11, 1910. The atmosphere, though it gave suggestion of the festive occasion, was laden with a heavenly fragrance. Strains of music floated over the scent-laden air as through the doorway walked Jessie and John, now no longer gay young lovers as in the days gone by, but bride and groom ready to step forth into the battles of life together, henceforth to know the same joys and sorrows, and to share the same perplexities and trials. Then and there they covenanted together and pledged themselves anew to Christ and His great cause.

So quiet and unpretentious had the whole affair been that some who lived in the school did not even suspect that a wedding was taking place, yet the marriage witnessed that day commenced one of the most perfect of unions.

The following two years found them engaged in evangelistic work first in the city of Urbana, then in Chicago, Tennessee, and subsequently in Canton, Illinois. Nothing was so captivating and enjoyable as the work of soul-winning in which he was now engaged. It was while he was laboring in the city of Chicago that a tall, fine-featured man of middle age stepped into the meeting one evening. He was a lawyer by profession and a man of talent and ability. The time had been when he was refined and cultured and drew a large income which provided every comfort. But he acquired the drink habit, and profession, home and friends were eventually sacrificed to the god of alcohol. Many times he had resorted to the so-called "drink cures" and had taken treatment at an institution for inebriates, but all his attempts to free himself from the propensity were futile.

He became, at one time, so desperate in his efforts to conquer his habit that, leaving his home and his practice, he sought refuge in a sparsely settled rural area where he thought liquor would be difficult to obtain. But, as he told Mr. Whipple, the only difference was that instead of a glass from a bar the liquor was drunk from a jug in a wayside tavern. He finally found himself in a big city far from home, a broken-down man, homeless, hopeless, and helpless—a captive to his habit.

But one night while still under the influence of alcohol he entered the Metropolitan Mission on Federal Street in the heart of Chicago. After the sermon, Mr. Whipple went back to where he was sitting and invited him to come to the Lord for help. He said, "I can't. I'm a hopeless wreck. I am past saving. I'm too wicked." Mr. Whipple put his arms around the man entreating him to let God take over his life.

There God met his soul as truly as the prodigal son's father met his wayward son, and from that moment he was a changed man. The chains that held him captive for so long were snapped asunder by the power of God. Not only was he completely freed from the drink habit but from tobacco as well. From that hour he enjoyed a peace he had never known and rejoiced in the liberty he had now in Christ. He was filled with the Spirit and for about a year and a half he lived to testify to the transforming power of God's grace. Then one day while helping about in the work of the small farm kept in connection with the Bible School, an elevator fell on him crushing his body beyond all hope of recovery. With a prayer on his lips he left this world happy in the consciousness that he was going to be with the Lord.

The Whipples preached the Gospel for the love of it and received no salary for their services. This sometimes occasioned hardships and sacrifices but after each time of trial on this line their faith was given a new impetus. God supplied their needs and they never went hungry though many times it required scheming and careful planning to make the money stretch.

One Saturday evening only ten cents was on hand to buy food for Sunday. But undaunted they took the ten cents and went to the store, Mrs. Whipple puzzling all the way over what to buy. Inside the window they saw some lovely peaches marked at five cents a box and then, she figured, they could spend the remaining five cents for some crackers, not a bad thought! Handing the money to Mr. Whipple she urged him to step inside and make the purchase; but no, he had never before bought five cents' worth of anything. He didn't mind asking for ten cents' worth of crackers or ten cents' worth of peaches, but what would the shopkeeper think if he asked for only a nickel's worth?

So crackers he bought and gave his whole ten cents for them and home they went, Mr. Whipple carrying a large bagful under his arm, for crackers were cheap in those days.

The next day—Sunday—found them munching away on dry soda crackers morning, noon and evening, and Mr. Whipple honestly confessed afterwards that while nearly choking on the crackers he longed many times for those nice, juicy peaches. This incident he often related as their first disagreement but times like these were few and far between during the happy years which followed.

In June, 1912, Mr. Whipple and his wife were again sent to Urbana to help conduct a ten-days' meeting, and they went gladly, hoping to lead some souls to the Lord. It was a great inspiration to him to preach to hungry people, but it was not always an easy task and many times the Tempter tried him severely; yet he held firm in his purpose to preach the Gospel and God's blessing attended his efforts. God had given him that promise, "My strength is sufficient for thee." He found it true.

During those meetings several people were born again and are carrying on as good soldiers of Jesus Christ today. At the end of the ten days a Jubilee was held and the crowd stayed on to the end. Many who before were bound by sin had found freedom and together they rejoiced for the things God had wrought. Shouts of praise and joy spoke of the happiness in their hearts and their faces showed that joy.

The tent was then removed to Champaign for a series of meetings and these were also blessed of God.

The tent was full every night and hundreds in that city had the chance to hear of a Savior who could deliver from the power of sin and set a person absolutely free. During this time God supplied their daily needs. Members of the little band there sometimes brought baskets of food for them and all these things they regarded as the hand of their God working for them.

But it was not all preaching and praying. During the day Mr. Whipple often helped in the menial duties around the house; he could scrub the floor, string the beans, or hoe the neighbor's garden as well as preach in the pulpit.

After a couple of weeks at Canton, Illinois, they returned to Wisconsin for the annual Camp Meeting there. Passing through Joliet where the state prison is located Mr. Whipple was very impressed. He wrote: "I felt especially thankful as we passed through Joliet and thought of the scores of lives that sin has blighted—of the hopes crushed and the disappointment of the young men whose lives are being spent in that gloomy place. I was very thankful to God for the blessing he has given me and my heart melted in praise to Him."

Chapter IV

A LONG FAREWELL

"With God go over the sea; without Him, not over the threshold."

TENDER LIGHT OF HOME BEHIND

The tender light of home behind,
   Dark heathen gloom before,
The servants of the Lord go forth
   To seek a foreign shore.
But the true light that cannot pale
   Streams on them from above,
A light divine, that cannot fail—
   The smile of Him they love.

The sheltering nest of home behind,
   The battle-field before,
They gird their heavenly armor on,
   And seek the foreign shore.
But Christ, their Captain, with them goes,
   He leads them in the way;
With Him they face the mightiest foes,
   With Him they win the day.

A wealth of love and prayer behind,
   Far-reaching hopes before,
The servants of the Lord go forth
   To seek a foreign shore.
And whereso'er their footsteps move
   That hope makes sweet the air;
And all the path is paved with love,
   And canopied with prayer.

            —*Sarah G. Stock*

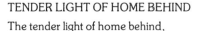

Chapter IV

A LONG FAREWELL

URING the Camp Meeting of 1912 the Rev. Charles Fordham, a missionary returned from Africa, spoke at one of the meetings. He told of some of the hardship that he had been permitted to suffer in the Gold Coast which at that time was known as "the White Man's Grave." He had lost his wife with the Yellow Fever so prevalent in Africa and he was compelled to bury her, as well as Brother Norman and another of their little band. He told how fiercely the enemy had assailed him telling him that the work in Africa would have to be closed and how God assured him that He would reestablish it and bless it. Then a missionary who had labored in India spoke, giving both the bright and dark sides of missionary work in the vast country of India with its millions of people still untouched by the Christian message. An announcement was made that a young couple was needed in India. To John this was a Macedonian cry that came not from the lips of the speaker but floated out over the waters thousands of miles from India itself. He felt that a great unseen Hand was being laid upon him to answer that call.

That Camp Meeting ended and little did the Whipples realize what a turning point it was to be in their lives. The Great Potter, into whose hands they had committed their humble clay, had been shaping and molding it into vessels He could use. He knew well where they would be most needed and just how to temper them for what was awaiting them in the future.

The day following the close of the meeting was memorable. Just as the morning meal was finished the Superintendent took Mr. Whipple aside into a corner of the long classroom and there broke the news that the Board was considering sending him and his wife to India as the couple they were so in need of. Oh, what a bound his heart gave! Could it be possible that he, once so unstable and faltering, could be entrusted with a mission so lofty, so holy? Yet he felt it was God's hand that was leading and he could only exclaim, "Surely God hath done wondrous things!"

That evening he walked out in the beautiful out-of-doors for a short stroll and it seemed nature never was more lovely. His heart went up in communion with God and a deep calm and sweetness stole over him at the thought of his glorious privilege.

But it had not yet been definitely settled and after that interview there followed a period of waiting and suspense. John in the meantime was sent to Chicago to assist in the City Mission there, leaving Jessie behind. He felt the loneliness without her yet found comfort in God and prayer. And, after all, was not this more training for the battlefield—for longer separations under more trying, more difficult circumstances?

This separation did not last long, as Jessie joined him a short time after. They returned to the Bible School about the middle of September. A cablegram had been received from the headquarters in India with the one word, "Workers." The need none could deny, but who should answer the call?

Mr. Whipple's face by now was set toward India and during those anxious days of waiting he often scanned the horizon and thought of that vast country and of its dark-skinned people now bowing to gods of wood and stone. He longed to go at once, and why should he be delayed? Why should they sit idle while millions were perishing? He had learned to pray and to "move the Hand that moves the world" and in his concern he turned to God. Strolling up into the woods one Sunday morning he knelt down and prayed earnestly that God would bring things to a decision—that they might go, and soon, if this was the plan for their lives. And God up in Heaven heard his prayer.

That very afternoon when the service in the hall was ended the Whipples were called into that parlor, now special because of those sacred marriage vows said there, where the members of the Board were assembled. The decision was made—they were appointed to India and were to leave in two weeks' time! They were not sorry for an unutterable longing had seized them to go and tell the glad tidings of salvation to their less favored brothers and sisters across the sea, from whence even then their mournful cries floated out over the waters and stirred their inmost beings.

October 11, 12, and 13 were memorable days— the days devoted to the Farewell Missionary Convention. In the Sunday afternoon service ministerial hands were laid upon Mr. Whipple in ordination giving him the sacred commission to "preach the Word." A co-worker with God, what a privilege!—a privilege denied to the angel throng but committed into the hands of consecrated men and women!

That evening he preached his farewell sermon on "A Living Sacrifice" and several persons present responded to the appeal to surrender their lives to God. The young would-be preacher, whose "knees shook both ways," now a minister of the Gospel!

That night little sleep came to his weary eyes. His thoughts were on the morrow and the many events that their last day among their friends and old acquaintances held for them. Next morning the little Green Cottage back of the school where John's brother Alfred and his family lived, was the scene of much emotion. After the breakfast was cleared away they all knelt down to pour out their hearts to their Heavenly Father above to ask protection for the travelers as they journeyed into a strange and distant land, and for comfort for those left behind. It was Alfred who prayed—only a sentence—and then he broke into tears; not an eye of that little family gathering was dry. Yet those were not the tears of sorrow, but home ties and friendships are not easily broken.

The last articles were hastily packed away, the last goodbyes spoken and they boarded the train which was with every succeeding moment to bear them farther and farther away from those they loved but whom they now counted not dear unto themselves for the sake of Christ.

But back in old New England there were more goodbyes to be said before they finally left their native land. As the Buffalo train sped eastward bearing them on their journey, their minds were divided between the friends they had just left behind and those so dear to them back in old Connecticut. But how differently everything would appear to them now from when they were lovers there in the days gone by. The same scenes met their eyes, to be sure; the same old friends greeted them in the streets of Quakertown village, but how different it all was now! No longer were their hearts set on a little home on a well-kept New England farm. They were strangers and pilgrims now with their faces set toward a far country. No longer did the old ambitions impel them but a constraining love for Christ and His cause drew them on.

While in Quakertown a great burden was upon John for the salvation of his old associates. In a gathering at an old friend's house, he exhorted them with much fervor to seek the Lord. In that little meeting eight expressed a desire to commit their lives to Christ and John was happy that he was able to lead them to his Savior.

Then came the parting with his aged father and mother, those so dear even after all the years of separation. His father was now very feeble and his form bent with the years of his long life. Could they dare hope to see him again? It seemed very unlikely and the goodbye was the last they expected to give him.

Leaving for Boston by the fast morning express they arrived at the port where their steamer, the Arabic, was moored and waiting. She was not long loading her cargo and was soon steaming energetically out into Boston harbor, then out into the great ocean beyond with her prow heading ENE.

Slowly and faintly the skyline of Boston faded from their view, and every moment the fact became more real that they had actually left home and friends and country—everything that the heart holds dear—yet not everything, for they still had each other, and what was more, they had Christ going with them and his cause like a great beacon shone brightly on the horizon. Meanwhile the noble ship was every moment bearing its precious burden farther and farther "from the land of their birth to the land of their great desire."

A week later found the Whipples in Liverpool, foreigners in a foreign land. From Liverpool they traveled by rail to Ustrad, the little station in southern Wales which was to end their journey for a time at least. Here they were met by Mr. Hollingsworth, one of the workers there, who escorted them to the mission house. Even here in the Rhonda valley waiting for the way to open to proceed to India the missionary spirit and the talents with which Mr. Whipple was endowed began to manifest themselves and it was evident to those about him that he was indeed a true missionary, even before he had the privilege of preaching in a non-Christian land.

Accompanying the Whipples was another couple supposedly on their way to Africa. They were irked at the delay in Wales and chafed at the bit in their impatience. They finally purchased tickets, boarded a steamer, and sailed back home. Not so with Mr. Whipple. God had brought him this far on his journey and he was perfectly willing that God should work out the remainder of his trip to India. Nor was this time of waiting idled away; Mr. Whipple entered into the work in Wales and his ministry was a blessing to those around him. In about a month's time money and permits were received to proceed to India.

Before leaving Wales Mr. Whipple received his ordination papers from America which had been delayed. To show how he felt at having this honor conferred upon him, we quote just a sentence or two from his diary: "Received my ordination papers today. It seems wonderful that the Lord would pick out poor me to bear the glad tidings; and yet that is just the way God works."

Chapter V

ON INDIA'S STRAND

*"That land is henceforth my country which most
needs the Gospel."*

—Count Zinzendorff

"To me remains nor place, nor time,
My country is in every clime;
I can be calm and free from care
On any shore, since God is there."

—Madam Guyon.

Chapter V

ON INDIA'S STRAND

T was a lovely December day when the S. S. Anatolia steamed proudly into Bombay harbor and the city loomed up in view. Out over the blue waters of the bay rose Malabar Hill with its famous Towers of Silence, and below lay the city with its colorful buildings and picturesque palm trees. It presented a scene such as only the Orient and tropics can boast. On the wharf were two anxious faces, fellow missionaries who had come down from North India to welcome the Whipples to India's friendly shores.

All was so new, so strange, yet so delightfully pleasing that they felt at home at once and longed to plunge into the work that awaited them. The natives with their curious accents and still more curious gestures both amused and drew pity from the heart of the missionaries. Oh, those first moments of contact with the Indian people! How Mr. Whipple longed to talk to them but his tongue was tied. He longed to tell them his mission but he must needs wait and pore arduously many weary months over strange sounds and articulations before his message could be conveyed. But during those days he learned the truth of the saying that "a smile is the same in all languages," and though he could not speak their language, he let them know he loved them and his heart was burning with a message of Christ and what He could do for them.

To one brought up in a western country there is nothing, perhaps, so fascinating as an Indian bazaar where dark-skinned shopkeepers sit cross-legged on the floor and artfully entice the passers-by with their gorgeous display of wares, and should one be disinclined to buy, the shopkeeper himself will stand in the street in front of his shop and call out, "Mamma, I got it! I got it!" And if the traveler from the west were not well-informed and alert, the shrewd shopkeeper would get two or three times the actual worth of the purchase.

What a contrast to the large department stores in some of our western cities! Some of the shops are scarcely bigger than an ordinary packing case and within this cramped boxlike place the shopkeeper sits with all the dignity of a king-emperor on an ivory throne.

After all the formalities of immigration and seeing their belongings safely through customs, they boarded the Bombay-Calcutta mail train. Twenty-four hours later they arrived in Allahabad just in time for the watch-night service with the missionaries there. From Allahabad the Whipples were sent to Jubblepur to help in some meetings that were in progress at that time.

Among those who attended the meetings were many Anglo-Indians as well as Europeans. The Anglo-Indians are descendants from the early settlers in India, most of whom worked on the railways, in the police, or in the government. It was among these people that much effective work was done.

One night while Mr. Whipple was preaching, a woman sat in the audience whose life was sad and unhappy. Her husband was addicted to alcohol and through its influence he not only deprived his family of the food and clothes they needed, but often in a drunken fit he treated his wife and growing girls most shamefully. As she sat in that meeting and listened to the message she felt convicted for her sins. Every word that came from the preacher's lips seemed meant for her and she wondered who had been the tale-bearer who gave him her whole life story. How like the woman of long ago who met Jesus by the well and then urged her friends to "come and see a man, which told me all things that ever I did." But the all-knowing Spirit searches the deep things of the heart and reveals them to faithful ministers.

That was the turning point in that woman's life. She gave herself to God that day and began to raise her family for the glory of God. Today, though she has gone to heaven, she has three children in missionary work around the world. (Also a granddaughter is now a missionary with the Wycliffe Bible Translators in Ecuador—Ed.)

Oftentimes soldier lads would step into the meetings and God mightily strove with their hearts. Several made a surrender to Christ and began to live consistent Christian lives. One young man who had been converted left that battery to join the missionaries and give his life to the work that God then laid on his heart. War broke out and most of the British troops in India were summoned away to the war, the Jubblepur regiment among the others.

The Monsoon is the Time for Plowing and Planting.

Village Women Harvesting Barley.

Oxen Treading Out the Grain.

Chopping Cane for Fodder

Beating the Husks Off the Grain.

Winnowing the Chaff from the Grain.

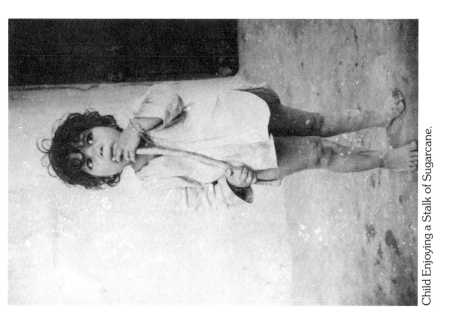

Child Enjoying a Stalk of Sugarcane.

Gleaner in the Barley Harvest.

How sorrowfully Mr. Whipple went to the station the night they were leaving to bid them farewell; and how earnestly he admonished them to be loyal to Christ and His cause at any cost. They went, but some never came back. One fine young man who previously had given evidence of a true Christian life fell in the war; another labors in a distant land while a third is endeavoring to preach the Gospel in his homeland.

It was a great joy to Mr. Whipple to see his labors blessed of God and people finding Christ. He would often stay up late at night after a meeting to help someone who was disturbed and needed God. Leisure time was spent in calling in the homes of the people or studying and preparing for his sermons. Only the Judgment Day will reveal the extent of the harvest from those years of sowing.

On the 30th of January that first year Mr. Whipple received a telegram announcing the birth of a son in Allahabad. He took this occasion to thank God and he prayed that this son should, likewise, grow up to honor God and preach the Gospel. He was given the name of Norman Emerson, a name made special by Brother Norman's recent sacrifice on the west coast of Africa.

Back in Allahabad Mr. Whipple was given the task of editing the little magazine they called the *India Burning Bush* so named in the hope that, as God spoke to Moses through a burning bush, He would use the new magazine to speak to many today. He never left the position of editor of this paper until he finally laid down all his earthly tasks. In this new job he was helped by the experience he had acquired teaching school in America. But each day he found new things to tackle and learn. Mr. Whipple began to study the Hindi language in earnest and applied himself with his usual diligence and faithfulness until in later years Hindi became as familiar to him as his own mother tongue and he himself often said he enjoyed preaching in Hindi with a crowd of Indians around him more than before an audience in his own native language.

One sad incident happened that first year in India that forced the fact upon Mr. Whipple that he was indeed in a land of many dangers and only a step from death at any time. Nightly during the hot summer months the missionaries had to sleep out in the open to get what little air might be stirring. The Whipples always slept at the back of the house just in front of a high hedge which shut off the servants' quarters.

One night they were awakened by a crying and groaning from the other side of the hedge. A servant had suddenly taken ill with cholera and in his agony he was crying out pitifully. Mr. Whipple was always sympathetic to another's pain and the poor man's groaning pierced him like an arrow. All through that long, dark night the shrieks of the dying man rent their hearts. Shortly after dawn his cold, lifeless body, wrapped in a bit of cloth, was carried away on the shoulders of some of his relatives down the road toward the sacred Ganges.

Up to this time while studying the language most of the contacts of the missionaries had been among the European and Anglo-Indian community, yet they knew their chief work lay among the Indian people and they were anxious to commence that work. And God had, as if to emphasize this fact, forced the native work upon them in the form of three little orphan children—Herbert, a boy of about eight years; Mercy, his sister, just two years older; and Florence, a wee brown tousle-headed girl of four. She was a starved child when brought to the missionaries and whenever a plate of food was set out for the dog, Florence would scamper along and share it with him. She soon learned what the dinner bell meant and fairly devoured the food set before her.

Each of these children had to be taught to read and write and be given the rudiments of an education so Miss Workman was appointed to teach the children. It was not long before they had learned to read and write and had added to their list of accomplishments such things as dishwashing, cooking, typesetting and sewing, and they became ready helpers in the household. Foremost of all, Miss Workman tried to instill into their young minds the principles of the Gospel and true and right living. Many, many times after a hard day's work she would sit and talk with them about the Lord and urged them to give their young lives to Him.

The following year the mission headquarters were moved to the village district of Siwait as we shall see in the following chapter.

کیونکہ خدا نے دنیا سے ایسی محبت رکھی کہ اپنے اکلوتا بیٹا بخش دیا تاکہ جو کوئی اس پر ایمان لائے ہلاک نہ ہو بلکہ ہمیشہ کی زندگی پائے۔

یوحنا ۳ : ۱۶

यूहन्ना ३ : १६

क्योंकि परमेश्वर ने जगत से ऐसा प्रेम रक्खा कि उस से अपना एकलौता पुत्र दे दिया कि जो कोई उस पर विश्वास करे वह नाश न हो पर अनन्त जीवन पाए।

For God so loved the world, that he gave his only begotten Son, that whosoever believeth in him should not perish, but have everlasting life.

Above is John 3:16 in Urdu (top) and Hindi, the two languages commonly spoken in the villages around Siwait.

Chapter VI

IN THE HEART OF A
THOUSAND VILLAGES

"If there is work he is there; if there is worship, he must be there. Happy is the place where resides the man who is not afraid of his share."

—Tibetan Proverb

This is the place called Imangah. Where are the hearts far
    departed—
Staunch, loyal and true, who came here and set up an altar
Like Abram of old in the midst of the desert about him;
Where God could be worshiped and blessed, then their task on
    earth all completed,
Upon that altar themselves gave life that life might be given—
Lit here a light to illumine and scatter the darkness
Of heathenish gloom, by satanic genius invented.
Imangah—the Place of Faith—the home of faithful endeavor;
God grant that true to her name, her sons may ever be loyal
And faithful to that trust—the care of souls immortal!

                    —*With apologies to Longfellow.*

Chapter VI

IN THE HEART OF A
THOUSAND VILLAGES

I T had long been a burden on the heart of Mr. Whipple and his colleagues to be out in a village district where they would have direct contact with the villagers—here, they felt, their true work lay. In a thickly populated area about twelve miles north of Allahabad there were several villages to which their minds turned and earnestly they prayed for guidance that God would direct them to the right one. A piece of land was procured—a site quite apart from any village or road, yet in easy access of many small villages and about a quarter of a mile from the Siwait railway station. But it was a barren site—only a *mahua* and one or two mango trees to shade the parched soil which was too dry for even a blade of grass to survive the terrible months of summer. No boundaries separated the fields, and the property was the common lot of herds of cows and buffaloes by day, and packs of barking dogs and howling jackals by night.

A tent was first pitched under the kindly shade of the *mahua* tree and Mr. and Mrs. Milligan and Miss Workman went there to camp and supervise the construction of the first building. It was not long before the villagers, learning of their arrival, flocked about and offered their services for a few annas a day. They were not experienced carpenters and masons to be sure, but master-mudmixers and just such crude workmen as are required to wield their crude tools.

To a westerner passing by there was not the slightest intimation that a building was about to be erected, for no piles of lumber, brick-stacks, or equipment were in sight, but promptly on signal that the work was to commence a group of half-naked men began to dig into the hard earth nearby. Water was poured into the hole and mixed with the feet until a soft doughy mass was produced. This was taken in baskets on their heads to the site of the proposed building. Layer after layer of mud was added, each being allowed to dry in the sun for a time. Then the walls began to rise, not entirely perpendicular to be sure, but in spite of irregular shape and crooked window frames and doors, the whole took on the aspect of a respectable bungalow. On these walls timbers were laid and a thatch of strips of bamboo tied with bits of rope and overlaid with *sarpat* grass. But this alone was not waterproof and the rainy season would soon be upon them. Gradually, as funds were procured, tiles were bought from a potter in a nearby village and to Miss Workman fell the task of testing these kiln-baked, clay tiles—5000 in all, each of which had to be tapped to make sure it was not cracked or broken!

The roof on and let it rain! In their mud and thatch bungalow they were happy indeed. What matter that the windows had no glass panes and in the middle of the day when the hot winds were blowing the windows were boarded up to keep out the heat, shutting out light too, so that no work could be done and they were forced to take siestas or swelter in the 120 degree temperature. But the new bungalow was still a palace compared with the tent where the sun beat relentlessly on the thin canvas and threatened to rob them of not only vitality, but life itself.

It was indeed a happy family that gathered in these first completed rooms. Several friends came from Allahabad, nearby villagers gathered around, and together they knelt and dedicated the building to God as His house, a place of His appointing for the spread of His Gospel. It was christened *IMANGAH* —the Place of Faith—and how appropriate the name! Each step of the building from the first layer of mud in the walls to the last tile on the roof, had been a step of faith. Henceforth, as we shall see, their faith was to be tested again and again in the trying years which were to follow. Late in June the monsoons broke and such rains! Never had Siwait known such a deluge of water. Miss Workman wrote the following in a letter back home:

"I am very glad to be back at my work again, although it is still quite difficult to get around among the villages on account of the floods. This district has had twice its usual amount of water this year and I do not think the rains are over yet. Mr. Milligan is out tuning pianos and a letter from him today says that where he was at that time, officers were going out in boats to rescue the people who had taken refuge in trees. Some villages along the Ganges have been completely swept away.

"This morning quite early I started across the fields to hold a meeting. I knew I should have to wade as

73

there is water all around us. It is rather dangerous because, while in some places the water may appear shallow, here and there are deep holes. Having taken off my shoes and stockings and strung them over my shoulder I was standing at the edge of the water wondering where to cross. A man who was cutting grass nearby came running to help me. He told me that in some places it was more than waist-deep and he kindly led me through the shallow part. Coming back I was able to get through alone as I remembered where he had taken me."

It was interesting and amusing to the missionaries to look out over the flooded fields during a heavy monsoon shower and watch the villagers—usually the *Pasis* —armed with their *lathis*, running down the big field rats that have been driven out of their holes by the rain. How their faces beamed as they trudged homeward, drenching wet, carrying two or three big rats by the tail, and anticipating a savory curry as reward for their trouble.

One day they noticed a group of children out under the *mahua* tree and went to investigate. There were four of them around a fire each holding a rat by the tail over the fire, fur and all, then munching away on their tasty repast.

In 1915 Mr. Whipple was given the superintendency of the mission. This necessitated the Whipple family which now boasted a new member—baby Alice —moving to Siwait which was henceforth to be the headquarters of the Metropolitan Missions in India.

There was much to be done in those early days. The type and printing equipment (at this time they did not possess a printing press) was brought from Allahabad and the process of setting up the *Burning Bush* was started in their new station. Herbert was then a lad of twelve years and to him fell much of the typesetting and making up of the forms which had to be taken to Allahabad to be printed, sometimes in an *ekka* drawn by a slow, half-starved horse. In the monsoons when the fields were flooded the trip was even more tedious. Each issue of the paper was a silent testimony of arduous toil and infinite patience.

There is nothing that binds hearts together like sharing hardships and sorrow, and so it was that during these years of recurrent testings and trial a warm friendship existed between Mr. Whipple and "Brother Milligan" as Mr. Whipple always liked to call him. No matter what the problem or difficulty in hand, Brother Milligan was always ready with a helping hand and could be relied on to perform cheerfully and whole-heartedly whatever part of the work was allotted to him.

Barefooted and with bare brown arms and face, he would come in from a long hard day's work in the fields trying to produce from that dry, barren soil something to feed the mission family and their oxen and buffalo.

But his weariness was quickly forgotten when asked to accompany Mr. Whipple or others to a village to proclaim a Savior's love. In the camping season when a few of the workers could be freed from duties at the bungalow they would go out with the tent into more distant places. It was heart-reviving to hear across the rice fields Mr. Milligan's familiar voice whistling a merry tune as he came to lend a helping hand in the meeting; then he would cycle back over narrow, rough footpaths happy in the joy of having spent his all unselfishly for the cause he so loved.

On one of these trips to the village of Barhaiya the missionaries made the acquaintance of Bipat, more properly and generally known in the vicinity by the name of Bhaktini. She had frequented the mission premises and her face was a familiar one to all, but now they were to meet her in her own little hut and her native environment. She was not a "holy woman" as her name would suggest—her friends' persuasion to become a *bhaktin* having proved fruitless—but still the name stuck to her and by any other name she would have been the same dirty, good-natured, hard-working, affectionate woman, and as hospitable (when funds would allow) as any New England housewife at Thanksgiving time.

She had had a hard life in her twenty or thirty (she never knew which) years of existence. Married at the age of about nine years she had been blessed of heaven—the Hindus called it cursed—with eight daughters, four of whom survived their babyhood. Then to add to her curses, her first husband had died which in itself proved that she was a wicked woman and to blame for his death. But Bhaktini bore all these sorrows bravely and loved her four little girls as tenderly as any mother heart ever loved an only son. She often consoled herself that, though sonless, *she had borne a son* —and her sad heart found a secret pride and comfort in having done so.

76

Her husband had been well-off, at least for a man of the farmer caste, so Bhaktini was left with a few small fields, a mud-and-thatch hut, and two or three mango trees standing on Government land! With this she was content; she did not want to marry again. But Baggar, also a farmer by caste and her husband's younger brother, eyed her day after day and made it known among the neighbors that he wanted to marry her. All his attentions were ignored and whenever he came and sat on her doorstep waiting for an opportunity to make his proposition Bhaktini would fly off to her fields and busy herself planting *jhundri* or sugar-cane, or watering or cutting her scanty crop.

By and by the neighbors began to jeer and urge her to marry Baggar. Was it from sheer persuasion, fear of what Baggar might do if rejected, or was it a secret hope that sometime, some day she might be the mother of a living man-child and the reproach of her lifetime taken away? Whatever the reason, she yielded and Baggar became her husband, not by any public ceremony—for this is unknown among Hindu second marriages—but simply by mutual consent and a feast given to all the caste members in its honor. But alas! what awaited her in the days to come she little dreamed of then, nor how dearly she was to pay for even the hope of what could never be.

North of the bungalow and about a half-mile from Bhaktini's village is Sarsa and there is Big Sarsa, Little Sarsa, and Ban-ka-Sarsa, or the Sarsa-of-the-wilderness. But it was in the first named Sarsa that Bedesi lived. He was a *Chamar* by caste and if he did the work common to his caste would spend his time gathering the bones of animals from the fields—the prey of vultures and long-starved pariah dogs—or working in leather, the two trades permissible to his caste.

But Bedesi appealed to the *Sahib* for work and had been working as a regular day-laborer almost ever since the first day at Imangah. He was a faithful worker and learned in the course of ten or fifteen years—it had taken fully that long—to buy a railway ticket, go to the city of Allahabad, purchase a few staples including meat, for his is the only caste permitted to touch beef, and find his way home again without any serious mishap.

Satna—little Satna—as he is called to distinguish him from another, much larger man bearing the same name who is also engaged on the mission premises, was *Pasi* (swineherd) by caste. He came to the mission as a mere boy and asked for work. There was something different about the lad from others of his caste. He was jet black, with quick, intelligent eyes, slim but nimble and very eager to learn. He was put at the garden work as the missionaries had no swine to herd, and slowly and steadily with the help of Mr. Whipple and Mr. Milligan he learned to set out tomato plants—foreign fruit—as the natives were wont to call them, make straight rows in the vegetable garden, make little canals for watering the fields; in short, he had almost become a first-class gardener. He taught himself to read and write Hindi and even taught his little daughter to read, a thing unknown in his particular community.

Among the older boys who used to attend the Sunday School was Bhagwandin, a tall bright lad of sixteen or seventeen years. Belonging, as he did, to the *Ahir* or the milkman caste, he was taken on as a regular servant to care for the oxen and the one milk-buffalo belonging to the mission. Bhagwandin became a steady, reliable man into whose care much of the farm and the management of the other servants was given. Working in close contact with him Mr. Whipple learned to love him dearly and in the chapters following we shall see how earnestly Mr. Whipple longed to see him a true follower of Jesus.

Up to this time all the water used on the mission compound had to be procured from a well a furlong or more from the bungalow. This was a great inconvenience to the mission family, as well as a source of danger from contamination. Villagers of all castes, dirty and clean, dip their *lotas* into the well, take their baths and wash their clothes at the well where it is not at all impossible for the dirty water to return to the well.

Mr. Milligan had tried to sink a well in one corner of the compound but when about half dug its sandy walls caved in and another site had to be chosen. This well proved a success. Water gushed up in such abundance that twenty feet of water remained in the well constantly through all the droughts and dry summers which followed. It still stands at Imangah, a monument to him whose great soul purpose was a passion to give the water of life to the thirsty souls about him.

Chapter VII

BEHIND MUD WALLS

"In the morning sow thy seed, and in the evening withhold not thine hand; for thou knowest not whether shall prosper, either this or that, or whether they both shall be alike good."

—Ecclesiastes

A Village Sunday School

"Sowing the seed by the daylight fair,
    Sowing the seed by the noonday glare;
Sowing the seed by the fading light,
    Sowing the seed in the solemn night;
Sowing the seed with an aching heart,
    Sowing the seed while the teardrops start,
Sowing in hope till the reapers come,
    Gladly to gather the harvest home;
        Oh, what will the harvest be?

—E. S. Oakey

Chapter VII

BEHIND MUD WALLS

ITH the labor and worry of the building work ended, the minds of all turned at once to the people in the villages about them, among whom they had come to minister. How their hearts rejoiced to have a place of their own right in the heart of Hindustan from which to give out the life-giving Word! As one of the missionaries expressed it, she had been in India for thirteen years and was just now getting her "heart's desire"—real close contact with the Indian villager.

One of the first happenings at Imangah was the opening of a Sunday School on the premises where the little brown urchins from all around came trudging along an hour too early on Sunday morning, laughing and chatting heartily or munching the last morsel of a hastily eaten breakfast. There they came that first Sunday morning—seventeen or eighteen of the most dirty, most charming youngsters you ever saw. Most of them were naked or scantily clad, the older boys wearing a loin cloth about the waist; a few of the girls had afforded *saris* but the smaller children wore the typical Indian dress: "a smile and a string of beads." And there was no age limit or classification in that Sunday School—old men attended as well as the babies not four or five months old who came astride the hips of their older brothers and sisters.

And how hard the missionaries worked to get even one little portion of Scripture into the minds of those children. *"Permeshwar prem hai,"* (God is love) was the little verse the worker tried to teach them but hardly a scholar retained it that first week. And sing? It was absurd that they could learn to sing! But perseverance and encouragement, sometimes in the form of a half-pice (one-fourth cent), accomplished a lot and today were you to walk though any of those villages surrounding Imangah almost before you realized that you were noticed, a chorus of childish voices singing a familiar Christian hymn or *bhajan* would greet your ears.

But work among the children was not all that absorbed their thought and prayers. Those villages were teeming with sorrowful hearts and the missionaries earnestly set about to take them the wonderful Gospel of goodwill toward men.

At noontime when the men would come in from their work in the fields and the women had done with their cooking, a little meeting would be held out in the village "square," which usually comprised a cleared spot of ground in the central part of the village, or the shade of a large *mahua*, mango, or *nim* tree. There, in faltering tones of a language both intricate and strange, the story of the Christ-child and His wonderful message would be told; that Christ who came, not to a western world but to Asia, is once again being presented to this bit of Asia as her Redeemer and Deliverer.

The sun beats down unmercifully but the missionaries go on with their story. Then as one by one the crowd begins to disperse, once more to resume their work in the fields, the meeting is ended and homeward the missionaries trudge, through the cane and rice fields, back to the mission bungalow.

At one of the meetings for the women of Badalpur they noticed a tiny baby with a bad eye. Inquiring what had happened to it, they learned that when the baby was only a week old a bit of straw had got into the eye and for five months it had been swollen to the size of an egg. All hope had been given up that the baby would ever see from that eye again and, instead of calling the child by a name such as other children have, they called her "Kani" (One-eyed). The missionaries told the woman that our Lord had power to heal the eye, and told her to bring the baby to the mission to have the eye washed and treated. There it was cleansed and bandaged, and for some time there was little result, but learning that the people were saying that this had come upon the child because she had a devil, the missionaries were stirred to pray more earnestly. Then almost before they realized it, the swelling in the eye went down so that the baby could open its eye. The eyeball was unhurt and the baby recovered fully. This was a time of rejoicing and thanking God.

The news of this baby's healing spread until in one week's time fifteen persons came to the mission bungalow with illnesses and begged the missionaries to do something for them. After their regular meeting in one village about a mile away they could hardly get away, so many besought them to help them with their bodily ills. They asked the Lord to draw these people to

Himself through the healing of their bodies as well as their souls.

Evening time, after the sun has set and daylight no longer lends her aid to the work in the fields, is another opportunity to converse and talk with the people. Tired and hungry, the farmers reach their huts; the oxen are fed, the long pronged rod used for a plough is safely deposited up in the rafters of the thatched roof, and they sit down to comfort themselves with their hookah while they wait for their evening meal. This often is served as late as ten or eleven o'clock, so the interval between while they sit and smoke, affords an ideal meeting time. A few notes on the cornet or the first strains of a hymn are enough to call the people who congregate around the singers and then listen to their words. A kerosene lantern or two are swung on the limb of a tree overhead. In its dim light can be seen a group of squatting, half-clad figures with earnest, appealing faces eager to hear the Gospel message.

Mr. Whipple was speaking of the Christian's hope of Heaven when an old leper who had listened very attentively spoke up and said, "Yes, but for all we know we may then be born a cat or a pig."

One of the ladies spoke to an old woman who seemed to drink in the truth. To the inquiry of whether she would forsake her sins and give herself to Christ, the woman replied, "If I accept Christ, my son will turn me out and then I will have no home in my old age."

Open-air meetings proved ideal for the hot summer evenings where meetings indoors would have been unbearable, but with winter coming on with its chilly nights, a new plan had to be devised. A tent, the gift of friends in America, was pitched in a small mango grove near Sadanganj, a village of considerable size. The tent was used for living quarters while out under the trees a log fire was made, straw spread on the ground, and a lantern hung, so the villagers could gather around and enjoy the warmth of the fire and listen to the message. A small folding organ or cornet and a few hymn books completed their equipment.

Peering out into the dim moonlight shortly after sundown—for in India there is no twilight—forms in groups of twos and threes could be seen in all directions heading for the tent. An advertisement is never needed to inform the people. News of the coming of the *sahib*, the tent and the wonderful "music box" is conveyed throughout the surrounding villages in much the same way as the news of the new circus just come to town is spread in one of our western cities.

After the meeting one evening Mr. Milligan inquired if anyone wished to ask a question; whereupon a man of the milkman caste asked who Jesus Christ was. Mr. Milligan was glad for this opening to tell of Jesus the Son of God who came into this world to save people from their sins. The milkman then related what he as a Hindu had to do to be forgiven of his sins. First he must bathe in the river Ganges, then choosing a spot of ground he must purify it by laying down some bamboo strips and then plastering them over with cow-dung. Then he must take a small image and after giving it a bath in milk place it on the purified spot. A Hindu priest then reads from the holy books and states the penance that the man must perform. "Then," said the milkman, "my sins are absolved."

Oxen Drawing Water from the Common Village Well.

A Typical Village Home and Family.

The Village Cobbler Mending Shoes.

Smoking the Hookah at End of Day.

The Ekka—a Common Mode of Travel.

The Popular Betelnut Shop.

Village Housewife Cooking Supper.

Shanti Grinds Spices for the Evening Meal.

"But," asked Mr. Milligan, "don't you commit sin after that?" "Oh, yes," was the answer, "then we must go through the same routine again." The missionaries tried to explain the Better Way and how through Jesus' death and atonement we can not only be saved from our sins but kept free from their bondage.

One evening when the crowd gathered late Mr. Whipple admonished them to come on time—and the time was usually designated by so long before or after the passing of the evening train. They told him they had been detained because Baggar had been beating his wife! Baggar hung his head when this was told and he gave as his excuse that Bhaktini had not cooked his food properly. Poor Bhaktini! She was already having regrets for having yielded to pressure to marry Baggar.

After the meetings, portions of the Gospels in Hindi and Urdu are given to those who can read, but in a meeting with thirty or forty people present sometimes there is not one who can read!

The meeting over, the crowd begins to disperse, and the missionaries are once more alone in the tent save for the few inquiring ones who remain behind to ask questions—too often not spiritual ones but: how much did the *Sahib* pay for his trousers; how does the music get out of the organ keys; how the *memsahib* combs her hair, and similar questions. When at last all alone, they kneel in prayer thanking God for the day and the privilege of ministering to these needy ones. Then in his diary Mr. Whipple adds at end of day:

"We had a beautiful prayer service together. God seemed very near. I felt a real uplift in soul and was impressed with the thought that never before under these trees or in these villages has the name of Jesus been heard in prayer or praise. Oh, what a responsibility rests upon us as God's ambassadors."

During the day their time was occupied in visiting villagers in their homes, preparations for the meetings, language study in both Hindi and Urdu, and their household chores. But of all the day's occupations none was so enjoyable as that contact with the people in their own mud huts. *Pasi, Chamar, Kumbi* and *Brahmin* — all were visited alike and a keen interest taken in all their activities. Below Mr. Whipple records a visit to a *Pasi* village. The *Pasis* are the swineherders and with the *Katiks* are the only castes of Hindus in that district that will eat pork. They are greatly despised by the upper caste Hindus but, strange to say, the Brahmins, in spite of their aloofness and prejudice, usually occupy a village, along with the *Pasis*, the Brahmins occupying the center of the village and the *Pasis* the outskirts. This is due largely to the fear the Brahmins have of an attack from robbers. The *Pasi* is brave and a stranger to fear and with his ever-present *lathi* (long staff, usually iron-capped) is ready at a moment's notice to defend his rights and his village. Thus they prove a great boon to the Brahmins and are after all indispensable.

Out on his daily visit one morning Mr. Whipple passed through a *Pasi* village and what he saw we will let him tell in his own words: "I witnessed a pig-killing today by the *Pasis*. First the pigs were tied by the feet and the place cleared and made ready for the *puja* (purifying ceremony). Then one man held a poor little pig up and another poured water over its head. A third man took a knife and beheaded the animal. After all the pigs had been beheaded the heads were placed on the prepared spot, adorned with marigolds, and while they were still quivering, the priest continued to pour water over them and chant as he did so. Then the priest bowed his head, did *puja* and the pigs were purified. They were then roasted *en masse* without removal of the entrails and the feast commenced. Alice and Norman who had gone up nearer out of curiosity were presented with some of the delicious repast and came back with their hands full of choice tidbits—pieces of intestines half-cooked, much to the astonishment and horror of their parents, while the poor *Pasis* thought they were giving them a great treat."

Under the date of December 11, 1917, still at Sadanganj, he writes:

"We had prayers in Hindustani in the morning. Satna went to the house and brought provisions. Herbert also went and got rope. The noon meeting was very interesting. A company of travelers from a village six miles from here came along on their way from the Ganges where they had been to bathe. They stopped and we invited them to stay for the noon meeting as it was not quite time. They sat smoking their hookahs and chewing *pan* (beetlenut) while we got ready for the meeting.

"They were very interested in Alice and Norman and gave them some little water jugs, some pounded rice and a lump of *gur* (unrefined sugar). When the meeting commenced they seemed very interested. The talk was on the prodigal son and they seemed to understand. In the afternoon I did some correspondence and went to the jungle to pray. I was greatly blessed in thinking of the great privilege conferred upon us in being able to give the Gospel to the heathen and the train of events that led to our being called into this work."

Before that winter of 1917-1918 the tent had been pitched in three different villages and, in the succeeding several winters they were able to hold meetings in all the villages of any size around them. It was Mr. Whipple's one great business here below to give out the life-giving Word. His only burden and sorrow was that more were not willing to accept the truth and this occasioned long intervals of earnest prayer out under the stars or in a mango grove praying far into the night. How like the Man of long ago who, after a long tiring day preaching to the multitudes, sought the solitude of a lonely mountainside there to make known His requests to his Heavenly Father and be refreshed in His spirit.

Chapter VIII

DARK DAYS

"Henceforth, then,
It matters not if storm or sunshine be
My earthly lot, bitter or sweet my cup.
I only pray, 'God fit me for the work!'
God, make me holy, and my spirit nerve
For the stern hour of strife! . . . and I joy
To tread the dark and death-fraught wilderness."

—Rev. Nathan Brown of Assam.

"Perishing, perishing! Thronging our pathway,
　　Hearts break with burdens too heavy to bear;
Jesus would save but there's no one to tell them,
　　No one to lift them from sin and despair.
Perishing, perishing! Harvest is passing,
　　Reapers are few and the night draweth near,
Jesus is calling thee, haste to the reaping;
　　Thou shalt have souls, precious souls for thy hire."

—*Lucy R. Meyer*

The Chowk—Allahabad

Chapter VIII

DARK DAYS

T is hard for one brought up in a modern western city with its conveniences and facilities to bring himself in imagination to a small, out-of-the-way Indian village with no post office, no motor cars, no telephones, and no stores from which to purchase supplies. Such was Siwait when the first missionaries made it their home with the object of teaching the villagers about a Savior's love.

In those days perhaps even more than now, times were hard. The trade between European countries was largely cut off because of the war (1918) and money was often delayed or detained altogether, so the little band of faithful laborers often had to endure real hunger and want. For months at a time not one letter from home was received and no money, so were it not for their trust in their Heavenly Father who fed Elijah in the wilderness and who feeds the sparrows, they would surely have lost heart and abandoned their enterprise altogether.

Brother Milligan, who felt the situation keenly, desired to help remedy their financial condition. He took short tours. tuning pianos, and selling books and *Burning Bush* magazines. This brought in some cash greatly relieving the pinch; yet in spite of all he did they were falling behind and their income could by no means meet their absolute necessities. Often in the hope of receiving a letter or a little cash through the mail, Mr. Whipple would cycle the full fourteen miles to the nearest post office in Allahabad, only to find nothing and cycle home again empty-handed.

Permit me here to draw aside the curtain and give you a glimpse into the everyday life of the missionaries at that trying period of their lives, else the picture I am attempting to portray would not be altogether true. God in His providence permitted each testing time only that the true worth of His workers might shine forth the brighter.

Lack of funds meant less to eat, less to wear and less to use in the spread of the Gospel. To cut down expenses they lived on rice and *dal* (pulse) and what Indian vegetables they could procure, which in the summer months were only onions and pumpkin. One meal would be onions fried and pumpkin boiled; the next, pumpkin fried and onions boiled, or, to vary the menu a little, pumpkin baked, mashed or made into pudding yet it remained pumpkin, and not the most nourishing diet at that.

One day when times were exceedingly depressing a bright thought came to Mr. Whipple. He was voluntarily taking a turn at getting the dinner and his ever-inventive mind served as well in the kitchen as in the office.

He had noticed the small white blossoms of the old *mahua* tree in the compound which the natives sometimes used for making *lapsi* and decided to make a *mahua* pudding. Surely never was manna in the wilderness more timely, he thought. Sugar was added to the *mahua* blossoms and the concoction committed to the oven and lo, after a few minutes out came a pudding which honestly and truly could have been termed None Such! Suffice it to say that to my knowledge a second *mahua* pudding was never attempted.

It will not be thought strange that such a condition soon began to tell on the health of the missionaries. Miss Huntington and Miss Workman both took ill with malaria, having fever on alternate days and, since there was no one to attend to their needs they were forced to take care of each other, in bed one day and up the next, looking after the house, the three orphan children and the patient!

Mrs. Whipple had given birth in the early part of the summer to twin baby girls—Marjorie Hope and Martha Faith. Marjorie survived though weak and frail but the other little one had to be laid in a tiny grave.

It was when Marjorie was still small that Mr. Whipple was taken ill with enteric fever so common in the tropics. At first he appeared to be suffering from a severe cold but he grew worse and symptoms of typhoid developed. Day after day the fever continued, rising higher and higher running without a break for six long weeks. It was evident that his condition was very serious and every effort was made for his recovery. A trained nurse was procured who did her best to pull her patient through; however, one day it became apparent that unless some Higher Power intervened they would soon have to lay Mr. Whipple away.

Daily, almost hourly, the little band of missionaries and workers knelt together in prayer asking God to spare his life. One night he felt the end was near. About two in the morning he called his family and friends to his bedside and gave them a few parting words and bade them all goodbye. When it came to Mrs. Whipple, the nurse said, "If you want to say anything to your husband you had better say it now for he cannot live much longer."

But Mrs. Whipple had been alone with God and she knew God was going to raise up her husband, so she refused to say goodbye. She believed God, and it was as God had told her. Suddenly a change came over him and he spoke to Mr. Milligan who all the while had been kneeling by his bedside; "I believe I shall yet live to preach the Gospel," he said.

Again Mr. Whipple's fever rose and during the next few days they were reminded by the nurse that he was a very sick man and they would have to pray, for there was no hope for him if God did not heal him.

Then came a further test. His fever broke but he remained delirious and got no sleep for three days and nights after which he lay in a stupor for about twenty-four hours. They began to pray that God would give him rest and he fell off into a natural sleep from which he awoke with a clear mind showing a decided change. Prayer was then turned into thanksgiving and praise.

Mr. Milligan wrote of this time: "It is true that 'God moves in a mysterious way His wonders to perform.' In his experience (Mr. Whipple's illness) God has taught us many lessons of faith. We had in years past seen cases of cancer, epilepsy, consumption and many other dread diseases healed instantaneously. It is comparatively easy to trust God when the answer comes immediately but in this case, how different it was! On March 2nd we received the witness that God would heal Brother Whipple yet he grew worse. The question seemed to be, 'Can you trust Me even in death? Since you have told others that Christ would be precious in the hour of death can you now say yes to God's will?' When the lesson was learned deliverance came. After passing through such severe suffering Brother Whipple said, 'Thank God, I now know that one can die without a single fear for the future.' Truly faith in God is more than a theory. It is more than a creed. It is a living reality. It is a personal experience which brings one up to the gate of eternity in perfect peace."

As new life came into his body, new spiritual energy was also given and Mr. Whipple came back to his family, as it were, from the very gate of Heaven. His work was not yet finished and God spared him to carry on the work he loved so well. Since change to the cool climate of the hills was considered necessary to his full recovery, in April Mr. and Mrs. Whipple were hurried off for a time of rest. He returned to the heat of the plains quite himself again and ready for the tasks before him.

Meanwhile finances continued very tight and the little band had to look to God for their daily bread. It was about that time Mr. Whipple records in his diary that someone had sent them twenty-two rupees, (about seven dollars) and he was thanking God for supplying their need! Seven dollars to feed a family of twenty!

Someone once made the remark, "What a hand-to-mouth existence!" "Yes," was the reply, "but when it's from God's hand to our mouth, it is beautiful." And so the missionaries found it and daily they found cause to praise God.

Even in the midst of such tight circumstances their thought was not of themselves but of the even harder lot of the poor villagers about them. Mr. Whipple was deeply affected by their sufferings and sought to further deny himself to share their suffering with them. A little example of this: he decided to eat his porridge without sugar to "sort of share with them" as he expressed it.

Cold weather was coming on and during those war days cloth was too dear for the average villager to afford. Mr. Sammons went to the Fort in Allahabad where the army supplies were kept and purchased four hundred-weight of blanket cuttings. These were sewn together into good-size blankets and distributed among the poor in exchange for a small amount of work. Miss Workman and some of the ladies cut up the smaller pieces into little coats, one hundred of them, to be given to all the Sunday School children. Thus a few of India's suffering millions were spared a cruel winter and some, perhaps, were saved from death.

Many young men from the villages had gone off to the war and it was pathetic to pass through a village and be met by half-starved bent old men and women, or a middle-aged woman with a puny, sickly baby astride her hips, inquiring from the *sahib* of a son or husband who had gone to the war. Two years had passed and no news had been received from them and no money. Dead or alive? They did not know and how could they when neither the one away nor those left behind could read or write? Gladly the missionaries endeavored to contact the husband or father and obtain a little news and financial relief.

Following the war there was the influenza epidemic. Villages once rife with life and thrift were now at a standstill, so many of the inhabitants having died of its ravages. The winter followed. Mr. Whipple writes of the village tent meetings: "Again we are having the privilege of recording Hindustani meetings in the villages. We expected to get started earlier but we are late due to the epidemic of flu and other hindrances. We do not expect that our meetings will be attended as well as last year on account of so much sickness and so many have died. It is indeed sad to hear of the awful inroads the influenza has been making in the villages. This morning I was out in the jungle and ran across three graves with the beds still beside them on which the corpses had lain. At the nearest village there is not a house in which someone has not died.

"Sunday we went out at noon to *Ban-ka-Sarsa,* the Sarsa-of-the-Wilderness, to sing and invite the folks to meeting. Quite a few people gathered about. After we had invited the people to the service a man insisted that we have some sugarcane juice as a mill was in operation nearby. I never saw a more interesting industry than was exemplified by a fat chubby boy of about seven years who, without a rag of clothing on, sat with all the dignity of an engineer driving the King's Special, feeding the cane into the mill. The juice served in clay dishes with ashes, etc. floating on the top was anything but inviting but we drank it anyway to please the donors. Three-year-old Alice took a sip and said, 'Me no like old sweet coffee!' "

Again under the date of March 20th he had written: "A poor old woman almost too weak to totter came from a village about six miles away. She claimed to have had no food for some days and from her appearance one could easily believe her story. Yet when offered some food she refused, knowing her caste would be endangered.

"Poor old Isri died yesterday and his sons took him to his last resting place, the Ganges, in the afternoon. The cook has just told me that a little baby boy was found in a hole just below our field. The poor little fellow was sucking his thumb when found, but he soon died from exposure."

November 20, 1918. "Our cook just lost his little eight-year-old sister from influenza. Before this, during the last six months he lost his baby, his wife from cholera, and his nephew from a snake bite. How many influences there are to hurl souls out of this world and into eternity, especially in this country. We feel especially thankful that during the past year with cholera, plague, and influenza raging at different times God has spared our little number."

Cholera broke out in a village about a mile away, so different kinds of *pujas* (ceremonies) were held by the men of the village. One evening an old man came to the bungalow begging for an old oil can, explaining that he wanted it to use it instead of a drum, to frighten away the evil spirits so that cholera would not come to his village.

Going to the village of Hajiganj to hold a meeting, the missionaries found the village deserted and the villagers living in straw huts on the outskirts of the village. The villagers knew of no way to disinfect their homes against the fearful plague epidemic, and to kill the rats which carry the disease would be sinning against the gods, so they built grass huts and remained in them until the danger was past.

During that siege of influenza one of the missionaries counted eighteen corpses floating under the Ganges bridge as she passed over. There was neither wood enough nor people enough to have them properly burned and the ashes cast into the sacred waters.

The love and sympathy he felt is revealed in these few lines of Mr. Whipple's diary dated December 12, 1918: "I have thought so much lately of the sufferings of these people. Poor souls! They for the most part have nothing but famine and pestilence and hardship and toil to contend with in this life, and nothing but darkness and despair to look forward to in the future. We do not begin to realize what it means to go hungry. Lately I seldom go to the table and eat until I am satisfied without thinking of these people who have only a few handfuls of grain with which to appease their hunger."

Under the date of September 26, 1919, Mr. Whipple has recorded: "We are in the midst of a very 'hot test' but the form of the fourth is seen in the midst of the fire. Our finances are very low (we owe a good deal) so at times we feel 'pressed out of measure' yet I am confident of His speedy help and victory. Today I went to Allahabad and as I had my Testament with me turned to it for comfort. These are some of the choice morsels with which God refreshed my weary soul:

" 'We are saved by hope: but hope that is seen is not hope.'

" 'And we know that *all things* work together for good to them that love God; to them who are called according to His purpose.'

" 'He that spared not His own Son . . . will freely give us all things.' We couldn't ask for better promises than these or for a better hope or a surer foundation."

But a trial far more severe awaited Mr. Whipple and one which cost him more personally than any he had been called upon to pass through. Mr. Milligan who had so faithfully stood at his side as helper, brother and friend, was called home on March 4th, 1920. In hopes of helping the mission financially, he had planned to sail for America. With his characteristic self-denial he proposed working his passage as ship's carpenter to relieve the mission of his steamer fare. On the day his boat was to leave Calcutta Mr. Milligan took ill and died after an illness of only a few days. How keenly Mr. Whipple felt this parting will be seen in a few lines from his diary written a month later.

"Our dear Brother Milligan has since been called to leave this earth for his own home in Heaven. It is the first time that a sorrow of this kind has ever entered into my life. For a few days I felt as though I was almost crushed but He who knows how to comfort the afflicted in their sorrow comforted me in my grief and in prayer I found great comfort and strength to go on in the fight."

Lest someone should fancy missionary life a romantic, easy career to follow we quote the following from his diary again:

"Monday - October 27th. Another day gone into eternity. It has been a day made up of little things. To a person with a sentimental idea of what it means to be a foreign missionary I suppose it would not seem so poetic as their idea of a missionary's life, but after all it is being faithful in small things that pleases God. This is how my time has been spent today—Got up about 6 o'clock; prayed and chose reading for prayers. Conducted Hindustani prayers and had *chota hazri* (early morning tea); saw about the work—how the men on the roof were progressing; made a list of type and things needed for Herbert to take with him; watered seed beds; saw to the workmen about sowing a field with *channa* (gram). Wrote mail, read English mail; had breakfast; was called away to pray for Miss Huntington who is ill; studied Hindustani, made out accounts, and recorded men's time, etc. Got baby to sleep, helped with the washing, had dinner, then family prayers in English. Will now read in my Bible and have secret prayer—One more day spent in God's service."

And those times of his secret prayer—some of us can remember well—were the life of the mission. Whatever new advance was made, whatever effort for the relief of the suffering or the spread of the Gospel, it was all born in those times of prayer and came fresh from God himself. It was in one of those seasons alone with God that Mr. Whipple made out a prayer list which comprised the following:

1. Orphanage Building
2. New Missionaries
3. Out-stations
4. Steady Income
5. Doors and Windows
6. Cow Stable
7. Conversion of Satna, Bhagwandin, Shabbar Hosain
8. A Hill House
9. Printing Press
10. Village School

Praying for doors and windows you may think a strange request, but for these three or four years since Imangah was built, summer and winter alike were trying times with nothing but canvas to protect them from the terrific *lu* (hot winds) in summer or the chilly winter days, though the latter were far easier to bear. Satna and Bhagwandin we have already made an acquaintance with and Shabbar Hosain we shall meet again.

Dark years they had been indeed, but the darkness was beginning to scatter. With faith's eyes the faithful soldier could look out over the horizon of the future and see the first faint gleam of a new day dawning. These lines of Cowper's were often on his lips as Mr. Whipple would quote:

"God's purposes will ripen fast
Unfolding every hour;
The bud may have a bitter taste
But sweet will be the flower."

News of reinforcement of new missionaries revived their hearts, and the prospect of launching out afresh in the glorious work God had given them imparted new courage and inspiration, and as they looked into the future, they were stronger, more earnest, and nobler for the trials undergone.

Chapter IX

HOME, YET FAR FROM HOME

"Breathes there the man, with soul so dead,
Who never to himself hath said,
This is my own, my native land!
Whose heart hath ne'er within him burn'd
As home his footsteps he hath turned
From wandering on a foreign strand!"

—Sir Walter Scott

"It is manly to love one's country;
it is godlike to love the world."

—J.W. Conklin

"Yet had his aspect nothing of severe,
But such a face as promised him sincere;
Nothing reserved or sullen was to see,
But sweet regard and pleasing sanctity;
Mild was his accent, and his action free;
With eloquence innate his tongue was armed;
Though harsh the precept, yet the people charmed;
For, letting down his golden chain from high,
He drew his audience upward to the sky."

Chapter IX

HOME, YET FAR FROM HOME

T was a hot windy day early in March of 1921 when the old *mahua* tree at Imangah welcomed travelers from afar—Mr. and Mrs. Varner, their little baby Virginia and Miss Ellen Callar. How good it was to see friends from the homeland, even though they were, up to this time, total strangers. They were fresh from a healthy climate and began their work with real enthusiasm and vigor, but before long death entered their happy family. Baby Virginia soon succumbed to a fatal hot-weather disease and was laid away in a tiny grave, saddening but not disheartening the parents who came to plant the cross of Christ in "regions beyond."

Money sent by the missionary classes of the Metropolitan Bible School and designated for the new orphanage building gladdened the hearts of the missionaries and another item was crossed off Mr. Whipple's prayer list. A suitable building was carefully designed and started, but no sooner had the foundations been laid before Mr. Whipple received summons to return to America, to arrive, if possible, in time for the Camp Meeting in August.

Building and the other work had to be left in the hands of the new missionaries and Mr. Whipple made preparations to sail for America, the land he had left so many years before; land of his childhood home where father, mother, and a multitude of loving hearts anxiously awaited him. In spite of the fact that he was leaving his wife and family and the work which he loved, he felt a sudden joy to think that once more he would gaze on the scenes of his childhood days and see those forms and faces which watched over him so many years, still dear and vivid in spite of long years of separation.

Passage was booked on the S.S. Orsova destined to land its cargo in London. London had many wonderful and interesting places to show this traveler from India but there was one place above all which held his interest—Westminster Abbey. There enshrined within its corridors are the tombs of such men as David Livingstone and Robert Moffat, men fired with the same spirit, the same passion for the spread of the Gospel that stirred within his own breast. What wonder then that he passed by the tombs of kings and monarchs and halted here, entranced, spellbound, vowing silently to follow in their train and work for the salvation of his Indian brothers while life should last.

From London he visited the little band of supporters at Heolycyw in South Wales where he had stopped as a young man while enroute to India. There a brother minister and old fellow-student of Bible School days lay ill and Mr. Whipple's heart was moved for him, and he sat by his bedside, ministering to his needs until he passed away some days later. John felt this brother's death keenly but rejoiced to know he had gone to be with his Savior.

The Camp Meeting in America was fast approaching and if Mr. Whipple was to arrive there in time he must leave Wales at once. Taking passage in a steamer bound for Montreal, he arrived just in time to make the hurried, over-land journey to Waukesha and arrive at the Bible School for the first Sunday of the series of meetings. Slipping in quietly in the very early hours of Sunday morning he found not a soul about. All was darkness and quiet, save for the night watchman on his hourly beat.

He walked down the long halls and corridors still familiar as in the old days. Yes, there was the place—he could remember it well—the room in the dormitory where Satan used to assail him and tell him it was no use; he might as well go home. And now, how thankful he felt! Each well-known scene brought reminders of battles fought and won, and down in his heart he was praising God.

But soon the news spread that John Whipple had arrived from India and then what a welcome! Hearty handshakes and tearful eyes told him it was truly genuine. But meetings were in progress and he was rushed away and ushered before congregations of thousands of his own countrymen where he must tell his story. It was not a hard-luck one. Days of suffering and trials on the mission field were forgotten. He had but one theme—the great need on the mission field and the privilege of filling that need. He was not sorry that he had answered the call and he could only urge others to do as he had done.

Yes, it was in a tent on those same grounds ten years before that he had heard from the lips of returned missionaries of those lands where darkness reigns, and God's call came to him. Could it be that there before him were young lives he might touch, someone to whom the call would come as it had to him in that meeting many years before? He earnestly hoped and prayed.

There was a charm about that preacher from the East, clad in the white *kamise* and *pagri* so typical of India. He had lost his youthful figure and the color of his skin was sallow and tanned by long exposure to a tropical sun. Even his accent was different and bore evidence of long residence away from his native land. But the people were charmed and even the most prejudiced against the missionary cause found reason to change his mind.

Can it be, thought some, that this is truly John Whipple, the young man they remembered from their younger days whose "knees shook both ways" when he first tried to preach and who ran away from the school from sheer discouragement? But he it was, and they could only marvel at the grace of God and what it could do for a wayward young man.

After Camp Meeting was over Mr. Whipple was wanted for meetings in the east near Reading, Pennsylvania. Those were the days of prosperity and money came easy to most Americans. Everywhere in his travels through the states Mr. Whipple was grieved by the extravagances for which money was being spent, and he would think of how far that money would go on the mission field. He took a pencil and wrote it all down: five cents for an ice-cream cone, that would furnish ten Gospel portions in Hindi, Urdu, or Bengali;

ten cents for an ice-cream soda, that would give some poor Indian villager a whole day's living for his wife, children and himself; fifty cents for a box of chocolates, that would buy six whole New Testaments in one of the vernaculars. It pained him to see the careless use of money that could be put to such advantage on the mission field, and he longed for the time to come when people would awake to the great waste in America and do something about it.

From Pennsylvania Mr. Whipple traveled eastward toward Connecticut, the scene of his boyhood days. At Millstone he found loving friends waiting to greet him—brothers, a sister, nieces and nephews—all anxious for a glimpse of Uncle John who had been so long lost to them except for a few letters now and then when his work would allow. Millstone days were quiet ones. There in that sleepy place that might well have been the Sweet Auburn of Goldsmith's *Deserted Village*, the tired missionary relaxed and gained strength for future battles.

Not a sound broke the quiet of that little New England village save the lapping of ocean waves against its rocky beach. Long shady lanes afforded him a retreat for reflection and meditation. And tall yellow golden-rod and purple asters waved their heads together in the autumn sun. He enjoyed his native clime and the association of relatives and friends, but a stronger love had taken possession of his inmost being. Often he would slip away from the family and wander down to a ledge overlooking the great expanse of water beyond, and he thought that these same waters wash that other land where darkness and death and the evil one reign. He longed to be again where he could reach these souls, where he could again proclaim the story of Jesus' coming into this world to save them. But the time would come—meanwhile he must wait and live for those about him who needed his message too.

Nor was he idle. Letters were written, missionary meetings held, articles written and sent to the India *Burning Bush*, and many conversations held with those who wanted to hear more.

About November the tidings came that Jessie had been summoned home and was en route to America and would land about the end of the month. Hastening to Boston, Mr. Whipple awaited her arrival. Early on the morning of the 20th of November, the S.S. City of Benares discharged its precious cargo. After many months of separation, the Whipples were united once more.

A meeting had been planned in Boston which would fall just at Thanksgiving time. How urgently his sister-in-law had pleaded for a family gathering at Millstone for Thanksgiving, a very human and natural wish, but Mr. Whipple would not concede. He was not the man to put personal interests first; in fact, he had no personal interests. Dearly as he loved his family he loved the cause of Christ more, and it was not hard to make the sacrifice.

When the meetings in Boston were ended the Whipples came once more to Millstone and planned to spend the winter there. Jessie's father was very ill and John voluntarily took up the task of caring for him. Daily he looked after the sick man's wants, read to him and conversed about many things. Mr. Crouch steadily grew more feeble and all knew that his passing could not be far away. He was greatly attached to John and when he prepared to leave for some meetings in Michigan the old man broke down and cried like a child. It would be hard to find another such a one to care for him. Who would read to him and sit at his side and talk to him as John had done?

Keenly as they felt the parting from one so close to the grave, they broke away and went once more for meetings in the West. At Ironwood God blessed their labors and there are those today who look back to those meetings as the turning point in their lives, when they ceased to live for the things of time and began a life of service to Christ.

Then followed a series of meetings throughout the Mid-west and the winter turned into springtime and springtime into summer, and still the meetings continued. The summer was fast drawing to a close and it was evident that if the Whipples were to return to India that fall refreshed and ready to resume their labors, they must have a time apart to rest and recuperate. Already Mrs. Whipple showed signs of a breakdown in her health from the strenuous round of meetings.

A little cottage on Lake Pewaukee was secured for them. Pewaukee is a delightful spot and the days spent there afforded opportunity for meditation and prayerful thought in preparation for the work· they would soon resume. But they were not too thus engaged to enjoy one another's company, nor to appreciate the beauties of nature around them. One memorable moonlight evening they were rowing on the lake together each helping with an oar. John remarked how well they rowed together and then spoke of how for nearly thirteen years they had pulled together in perfect harmony. July the eleventh would complete thirteen happy years of married life. Friends took advantage of the occasion and planned a celebration which would commemorate their anniversary as well as be a farewell gathering, for before many days they would again be leaving for a foreign land.

The lawn south of the Fountain Spring House was decorated with gaily colored lanterns swung from the trees. The combined Young Men's Missionary Class and the Young Ladies' Missionary Class together with many old friends and new, gathered that evening to offer their congratulations and to bid the Whipples God-speed on their errand of service to India's millions. They were farewelling the missionaries to a land of disease and death, a land hostile to the westerner's frame. Would that land be gracious and spare them once more to visit their native shores? It seemed unlikely; too many had already succumbed and they themselves had seen too many of its ravages to hope that they would be spared. Yet they were glad to go as they realized the time of their departure was nearing. Once more they were leaving the land of their home for the "land of their hearts' desire."

It was nighttime and softly and sweetly over the night air came the strains:

> "Carry the light, the soul-cheering light,
> Into the night—the dark heathen night;
> Tell them the story of Christ and His glory,
>   The One who is mighty to save."

120

And the darkness about them seemed to speak of the greater darkness to which they were going. Here they were surrounded by friends, in a Gospel-lighted land; in a short time they would again be alone in a foreign land and there, with their God, would have to battle against the powers of spiritual darkness.

But Mr. Whipple's heart was there and he express-ed his feelings in the song which he sang:

"Oh, I'll soon take up my duties
In that land so far away;
Even now the thought my soul with rapture thrills.
So goodbye, my friends and loved ones,
For the time has come to go;
I must leave you for the dear old battle-field."

One of the Youngest Pupils in our Village School.

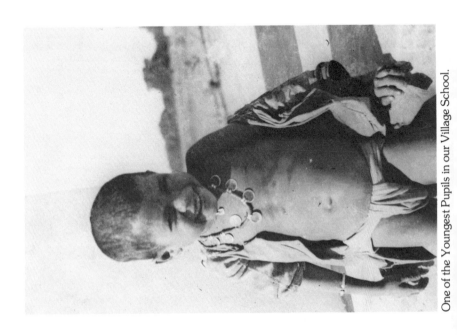

Dulari's Family Belong to the Milkman Caste.

The Village Mosque.

Mohammedan Praying.

Elderly Maharoo and Mewar Hill men of Sua-poli Hill

chenjunga as seen from Darjeeling.

Taj Mahal in Agra.

Chapter X

BEAUTIFUL HIMALAYAS

"Get thee up into the high mountain . . ."
> —The Prophet Isaiah.

"Great things are done when men and mountains meet;
This is not done by jostling in the street."
> —William Blake

Tibetan Prayer Flags

Mountain Sanctuaries.
           No minsters rise
Like them in pure communion with the skies,
Vast, silent, open unto night and day;
       So might the o'erburdened Son of man have felt,
       When turning where inviolate stillness dwelt,
He sought high mountains, there apart to pray.

—*Felicia Hemans.*

128

Chapter X

BEAUTIFUL HIMALAYAS

HE year following the return from furlough was a hard year. Added to the burden of the work Mrs. Whipple suffered a serious breakdown which for months kept her confined to bed. But the activities of the mission must go on. Mr. Whipple wanted very much to branch out. Tent meetings were opened in Allahabad and these occupied a good deal of Mr. Whipple's time during the winter of 1924-1925. After the series of meetings were ended Mr. and Mrs. Varner were asked to take charge of the mission there in the city to shepherd that flock. But a smallpox epidemic had broken out in the city and Mrs. Varner, who with her whole soul had assisted in the mission, contracted the disease and succumbed.

The loss of a much valued worker like Mrs. Varner was keenly felt by all. But missionaries in isolated places cannot stop long to mourn even a loss so great. The necessity of removing the small children to the hills was apparent. Baby Frances, now motherless, was only five months old and her brother, Robert, just two years older. Then God touched the heart of some Finnish missionaries in Ghum up in the Himalayas, who opened the doors of an old mission house, now no longer needed for their own use.

Ghum is a delightful spot situated at an altitude of 7,400 feet on the Darjeeling-Himalayan Railway and just four miles from Darjeeling itself. Old Mission House sits by the side of the main road leading to Darjeeling. It boasts no spacious lawns, no trees or hedgerows. It is merely edged in between the steep valley at the back and the roadside in front—yet it would be difficult to find a prettier, more picturesque scene than that looking out over the Himalayas from Old Mission House. Green, tidy tea gardens dress the hillsides in the valleys, and higher up tall cypress and evergreen trees stand like sentinels guarding the citadels of the snow-clad peaks. Through the treelined vista Kanchenjunga rises majestically like an oriental potentate clothed in ermine, commanding and receiving silently, admiration from travelers from every part of the world.

To vist Ghum is to visit both Nepal and Tibet in miniature. It is situated right on the borderland of Nepal and only eighty-five miles from the great "roof of the world," the vast country of Tibet. Here travelers from both of these countries come to trade, some of them remaining more or less permanently.

One does not have to wander far from Old Mission House to see symbols of a religion as complex as any on God's beautiful earth. The religion of Tibet on the Indian side is Buddhism combined with Lamaism (priest worship), idol worship, and devil worship all together, and most of the religious acts performed are done to appease evil spirits. Small huts dot the hillsides and in front of each, one or more prayer flags on long poles may be seen floating in the breeze. If you were to examine one closely you would find it inscribed with

130

queer characters which make up the prayers that are wafted by the breeze up to the Great Spirit to seek his favor.

Another device and substitute for prayer is the prayer wheel which every lama carries about with him and even lay Buddhists use morning and evening at the time of their devotions. Old people sit the whole day turning their prayer wheels as their last hope for a good rebirth in the next life.

The prayer wheel consists of a round hollow brass box fastened to the end of a piece of bamboo with a weight on the end of a chain that serves as a propeller to turn the wheel on its pivot. Inside the hollow box is a piece of paper on which prayers are printed. Very devout lamas may be seen at all hours of the day twirling their prayer wheels round and round, at the same time counting their beads. All the while the devotee repeats the syllables, "OM MA NI PAD MI HUM," which represents the six regions in the wheel of life into which each soul is born and reborn, until at last it is absorbed into Buddha himself and from thence into Nirvana, or the great void and state of nonexistence, the desire of every Buddhist.

Mr. Whipple's heart yearned over all who were still in spiritual darkness, be they Nepalese, Tibetan, Assamese or the dark-skinned Indians living in the villages he knew so well.

One day strange sounds were heard in the bazaar and, rushing out to learn the cause they saw, amid a turbid throng of brilliantly dressed Tibetans, a large packing case being carried through the streets on the shoulders of four coolies. Drums were beating, bells ringing, and weird incantations sounded by the priests who led the procession. It was not a wedding nor a New Year's festival but the funeral of a well-to-do Tibetan storekeeper who had long been a familiar figure in the Ghum bazaar.

A strange belief exists among these people that if a corpse is put in a sitting position as that of a Buddha, great gain in the next life is assured and should one be so fortunate as to die in that position still greater bliss will be enjoyed. In the life to come he will be reincarnated at once into one of the highest beings and escape the intermediate regions of torture and pain. So they carried the corpse along through the streets upright in the huge packing case, gaily decorated with canopy and colorful cloth. It was a scene one could not easily forget.

The Tibetan lama is always an object of interest to an outside visitor and may be seen almost any day along the roads of Ghum bazaar. Lama, or *blama* as Tibetans would say, means *chief,* or the *highest.* He is supposed to have mysteriously escaped the wheel of life and the "never ending pain of reincarnation," yet the lama is often far from a saint. Lhasa, the "place of the gods," is supposed to contain more than 16,500 lamas, the head of all being the Dalai Lama, a living Buddha, who is worshiped by all good Tibetans.

In the Tibetan home the woman is the manager, the earner, the mother, housekeeper and often has to pose as protector for her husband. Her duty is to be strong and hardy and we have seen her pass by with a huge trunk on her back, holding an umbrella over her husband who calmly walks by her side unencumbered.

One day while walking along the Darjeeling road Mr. Whipple noticed by the wayside a small shelter built of sticks and green twigs. Inside the little booth a platform had been erected which served as a sort of altar, and upon this altar there were several small offerings—a few grains of corn, a small quantity of rice, bits of bread, and among them an egg shell and some chicken feathers.

Some time afterward, while in conversation with a young Tibetan, Mr. Whipple told him what he had seen, and being curious to know what part the eggshell and chicken feathers played in the sacrifice, he inquired for what purpose they had been offered. "Oh, they were for the gods to eat," the lad replied with a grin.

Mr. Whipple took this opportunity to speak of the requirements of the Gospel: "The Tibetan's god may be satisfied with an empty shell and a feather offering but the living God never. He requires our all or nothing. It is impossible to rob God and enjoy soul prosperity. He spared not His best, and nothing short of our best is acceptable to Him."

Late in that summer spent in Ghum another little life was sent to gladden the Whipple home, a baby brother whom they named Earle. Mrs. Whipple's health was poor, and a winter in the hills, they felt, would do her good, as well as be of inestimable worth to those growing children. So the children, their teacher, and Mrs. Whipple spent that one winter in Ghum, studying their lessons and enjoying the snow and ice which the children now saw for the first time in their lives.

Spring came and a move was made to Edenvale at Tung, a station about eight miles further down the mountains on the same railway. Edenvale was ideal for the large mission family. It had been a tea estate manager's bungalow, with spacious lawns and tall pine trees.

One day in June a man, poorly clad, approached Edenvale with a child astride his hips and a basket on his back. His flat face and almond eyes pronounced him Tibetan or Bhutanese, or a mixture of both. Setting the basket down on the doorstep he sighed and sat down to rest. He appeared ill and all thought he had come to ask alms in the usual way. But no, he was asking for nothing and when Mrs. Whipple inquired his errand he pointed to the basket. Yes, there was the basket, but what could he be wanting? What could she want with those dirty rags? She looked again; she thought she saw them moving. There underneath that mess of rags and vermin she saw a naked, half-starved baby.

He told her a sad story. He had had a happy home but trouble came. His wife died leaving these two small children and he, unable to procure milk and food for them, had come to ask the missionaries to take his child—the younger one. The older child, a boy of about two years, he could not give away—at least not now—for he was ill and his religion forbade him giving away a sick child. If it recovered, he promised to bring it one day. Neither the father or the child was ever seen again.

The wee baby girl was taken in and a home made for her, but only after a thorough cleaning up time and much soap and water. She was not a pretty child but all that houseful of children flocked to admire the new baby and all were willing to contribute some article of clothing or volunteer to nurse her after school time. Phul Maya made the sixth child in the family and Niwa Manji arrived just a day later making seven. He too was brought to the missionaries by his father who was Nepalese. In after days when Niwa and Phul Maya were older they became great friends and used to call each other brother and sister though one is Nepali and the other Bhutanese.

During most of that year Mrs. Whipple continued in very poor health which was an added burden for Mr. Whipple. In those times when pressed by things around him he went to a quiet spot alone with God and then came back with renewed energy and a heart as light as a child's.

It was one of those depressing days and it fell on a Sunday. Mr. Whipple chose for his text that Sabbath morning: "Is there any sick among you, let him pray; is any merry, let him sing psalms." He applied it to their own lives and in many more dark days to follow he lived that sermon daily before his co-workers—truly a living epistle—and all who knew him remember him as one who rejoiced evermore, prayed without ceasing and was never known to murmur at the hardest circumstance.

Chapter XI

THE MAGH MELA

"I'd rather see a sermon than hear one any day;
I'd rather one should walk with me than merely tell
the way."

—Edgar A. Guest

"Only like souls I see the folks thereunder,
    Bound who should conquer, slaves who should be kings;
Hearing their one hope with an empty wonder,
    Sadly contented with a show of things.

Then with a rush the intolerable craving
    Shivers throughout me like a trumpet call,
Oh, to save these, or perish for their saving,
    Die for their life, be offered for them all!"

The Magh Mela at Allahabad

138

Chapter XI

THE MAGH MELA

T is just twelve miles by rail or fourteen miles by road to Allahabad from the mission bungalow at Siwait. Allahabad, "the abode of the gods," is one of the oldest cities in India and the one-time capital of the government of the United Provinces of Agra and Oudh. Allahabad is a sacred spot to the Hindus as it is the site of the confluence of the three rivers, the Ganges, the Jumna and the Saraswati—the last an underground river, or so it is said. Not far from the confluence of these rivers rises an ancient fort which was built by Akhbar the Great in 1575 and ceded to the British in the year 1801. Within the fort an interesting feature is a stone column thirty feet high which was built by the Buddhist king Asoka about the year 240 B.C. It was now being used as a place of exile for a Nepalese royal family and the sight of the high stone walls overlooking the river presented an awesome picture.

Below the fort stretches a plain which reaches down to the confluence of the rivers and which, in the rainy season, is overflown with a deluge of water from these rivers. They have their source far up in the Himalayas and carry with them the surplus rain and melted snow. Once a year, usually in January—the month Magh in the Hindu calendar—Hindus from all over Asia and even from Africa come here to bathe in the sacred waters. Were you to stand on the walls of the fort at the time of the Magh Mela and look down on the plain below, it would appear a turgid sea of thousands of human beings surging to and from the sacred Ganges.

The days of the new and the full moon, as well as any lunar or solar eclipse, are very auspicious for the Hindus and special merit is accorded those who bathe on these days. Then once every twelve years is held what is known as the *Kumbh Mela* when the number of bathers reaches a million or more. There is one day above all the others which is regarded as most propitious, and the hour of sunrise, especially the few moments when the first rays of the rising sun appear over the waters, are particularly so.

For miles around, sixty or seventy-five perhaps, each highway, road and footpath is a living stream of pilgrims all headed for that one sacred spot, to arrive, if possible, at that one most sacred moment. Is it small wonder then that in the awful rush many hundreds of lives are lost each year? Old decrepit men and women are trampled to death in the mad rush to reach the waters in time, but these are only regarded as very fortunate in having died on the banks of the holy river, Ganga Mai (Mother Ganges), and at such an auspicious moment!

It was at the time of the twelve-year Kumbh Mela in 1930 that Mr. Whipple had occasion to travel by motor to Fatehpur, seventy-five miles on the Allahabad-Kanpur road. Band after band of pilgrims was passed, and ox-cart after ox-cart laden with women and children from the more distant towns and villages all headed for the one sacred spot, the confluence of the rivers. Not until Mr. Whipple had passed the seventieth milestone was the road clear enough to travel safely. All this only increased the burden on Mr. Whipple's heart and he formulated a plan to reach as many of these pilgrims as possible with the Gospel light.

Phaphamau is the railway station at the north end of the long bridge spanning the Ganges river and where all trains leading to and from Allahabad must stop. Here three lines converge, one leading to Lucknow and places northwest, one north to Fyzabad and one to Jaunpur and towns to the northeast making it a focal point for traffic. To add to the congestion the Allahabad-Lucknow road also meets the railway at this juncture.

Mr. Whipple felt this would be a good place for headquarters for the colporteur band for the duration of the mela and he had a tent erected not far from the station where the workers could replenish their supply of tracts and Gospels and refresh themselves when needed. From this point they would fan out, some working the trains headed for the mela in Allahabad, some the trains arriving from Allahabad, while others stationed themselves on the road leading up over the bridge where ekkas, tongas, ox-carts, camels and pedestrians jostled one another in their haste and anxiety to reach the sacred confluence at the proper time.

141

They sold Gospels of Matthew, Mark, Luke and John in Hindi and Urdu for one pice each (one-half cent) and distributed both Hindi and Urdu tracts free to all who could read. All through those long hot days the colporteurs would sell, Mr. Whipple when free from other duties, taking the lead and always the most enthusiastic seller of the crowd.

When evening came and darkness fell, the pilgrims stopped by the roadsides and in nearby groves to camp for the night and prepare their evening meal. By the light of their campfires when the tired, wayworn pilgrims had sat down to rest, the missionaries would join the group. A little friendly conversation as to where they lived, news of their families, their occupations, etc. and the missionary was made to feel right at home. The Indian is a lover of music so the suggestion of a song or *bhajan* is met with a cordial welcome.

There under the stars around these pilgrim campfires the wonderful Gospel story is sung and told again and again, from one group to another, until at last the tired missionary wanders off in the direction of the tent. Meeting with the others of the colporteur band the money is collected and counted. Seven hundred pice! That means seven hundred people will read of the plan of salvation and the story of Jesus, and seven hundred homes will possess a portion at least of the Word of God as the result of that day's labor, and only Heaven will reveal the final results.

Here in the mela crowd were all castes and classes of people and some would on occasion try to hinder the selling. Snatching a Gospel from a missionary's hand, an educated Hindu cries out to the crowd, "The

142

Christian religion for a pice! What kind of religion can this be to sell so cheap?" Some of these would go about through the crowd threatening the people if they dared to buy, even snatching copies from those who had bought and tearing them up.

In one area people were buying readily. Dozens had already been sold and quietly, unassumingly the workers slipped about through the crowd endeavoring here and there to sell a few more, always keeping one eye open for anyone who should be following them and trying to stop the selling. Out from a side path stepped just such a man who snatched a Gospel and, lighting a match, he quickly set fire to it, calling out to the crowd as he did so, "Yih kaisi kitab jo ap se ap jal jati?" (What kind of a book is this that burns itself up?) After being thus intimidated nothing could persuade the would-be buyer to buy while these men were looking on, but slipping around quietly after all the commotion had subsided, he proffered his pice and tucked his newly acquired possession carefully under his waist coat.

So is it small wonder that the party rejoiced that they had sold seven hundred Gospels that day? Mr. Whipple was never easily satisfied having gone over an area once or twice. Over and over again he would edge his way through the mela crowd dodging the ox-carts, cycles, and camels, finally finding his way back to the tent tired and thirsty.

In the evening after the sun had set and darkness had halted the work of selling, the missionaries wandered back to the tent where there usually was a crowd gathering to listen to the singing and preaching which went on into the night.

One night a young Brahmin walked into the tent. He had purchased a Gospel of John at Phaphamau station the day before while en route to the mela grounds. His mother had died recently and he was making this journey to propitiate the gods for her sins and assure her peace in the after-life. Sizing him up the priests had demanded that he pay for a large number of cows at twenty rupees each. He acquiesced, bathed in the river, paid the priests, did his *puja* and then tired and sad, he sat down to rest by the wayside. He pulled out the little booklet he had purchased the day before and began to read. Somehow the Spirit of God illumined his mind and he knew there was a better way to salvation than what he had gone through that day. He resolved he would go back to Phaphamau station and try to find the foreigner who had sold him the book. He followed the course of the river by foot, crossed the long Ganges bridge and arrived at the station weary but eager to find the colporteur. He was not hard to find with his white face and western clothes; he stood out even in that large mela crowd. Together the two walked over to the tent where a meeting was already in progress.

Mr. Whipple was preaching about salvation. It was not obtained by doing penance or puja or bathing in the Ganges but by accepting Jesus Christ who has already atoned for our sins by his death on the cross. The young Brahmin was struck to the heart. "Why," he said, "I have just been to the Ganges and I have given a large offering to the priests, and I found no peace. Now I know salvation is a free gift and that it is for me." Tired as he was he began to ask for this gift and then immediately jumped up, thanking God for deliverance from his sins. He had found Christ and let Him come into his heart. He asked Mr. Whipple to cut off his *chutiya,* the lock of hair that is a symbol of Hinduism. Then he spoke before his fellow Hindus urging them to accept Christ.

Mr. Whipple talked to the young man about staying over for a few days to get better acquainted and learn more of the Christian faith. He knew that he was facing possible persecution in Nepal but he said that he must return to his home as his leave from his government job was up. That night he boarded the train headed for Nepal taking a number of books and tracts with him.

About eight days later Mr. Whipple received a telegram from the young man saying he was having some difficulty and needed some money to get away. Mr. Whipple sent the money at once fearing he was undergoing persecution and had probably lost his job as a result of his conversion. Prayers went up for him that he would remain true to his Lord and be able to witness to his family and village. Within a week the telegraphic money order was returned with one word scrawled across it—"DECEASED."

Chapter XII

IN THE FOOTSTEPS OF
THE GREAT HEALER

"Is there no balm in Gilead;
Is there no physician there?"

—The Bible

"I stand by the side of a current
    That's deeper far than the sea,
        And the storm-beaten craft
        Of every draft
    Come in to be healed by me.
And some have more sin than sickness,
    And some have more grief than pain;
        God help me make whole
        Both body and soul
    Before they go out again."

Chapter XII

IN THE FOOTSTEPS OF
THE GREAT HEALER

H IS must be a stony heart indeed who can look on another's suffering and not be moved by it. Christ was touched with the feeling of our infirmities and the record of his ministry here on earth is a record of His going about doing good and healing the sick. Almost daily for years the villagers had passed through the Siwait mission compound stopping to tell their tales of suffering to the missionaries. Scarcely ever have they gone afield but some poor maimed, sick and infirm villagers would accost them seeking a little medicine for their ailing bodies.

In the village of Barhaiya a poor old woman had been gored by a buffalo—the animal's horn having torn the abdominal wall, causing a severe wound which had become septic. Daily one of the missionaries walked to her village to attend to her wound, dressing and keeping it clean, and usually reading a portion of the New Testament to her and teaching her to pray. In a few weeks she recovered and the news spread far and wide. It soon took one of the missionaries an entire morning to care for the ones who came for treatment.

Having no suitable place available one corner of an already over-crowded storeroom, where the supply of charcoal and laundry equipment was also kept, was used as a dispensary and some fifty or seventy-five patients were cared for daily. It was very evident that a place larger and more sanitary would have to be built and devoted solely to this work. So Mr. Whipple began to pray and to plan for it.

One morning an old man trudged into the compound looking weak and debilitated and carried a large dirty rag in his arms. One of the ladies who had had some training was caring for the patients that day. She thought he was carrying a baby in those rags, and since it was not crying, she was going to let him wait his turn. Then he staggered and she thought he was going to faint. She caught him just as he let his arms drop to his side and there inside those rags were several feet of squirming intestines. He had also been gored by his buffalo and the wound was covered with straw and the dirt into which he had fallen.

She cleansed the area, replacing the intestines and poured some home-made sterile saline solution into the wound. Then a quick thought came to her and she sprinkled into the wound some white powder sent out by a pharmaceutical company to try out in just such cases—a powder that as yet was known only by a number, M & B 693. She inserted a sterile Penrose tube, and had him put in Fowler's position to drain. A cot was placed on the veranda as it was evident he could not return home yet. He healed nicely with no sign of infection! This was the first they had heard of antibiotics; it was the beginning of great things in the treating of patients. How they thanked God for it!

Another old man came at about the same time who had a very septic foot—the whole top of his foot had been eaten off by a turtle while bathing in the Ganges. He was treated and also had to be given a cot near the storeroom as he was unable to walk back to his village.

All of these patients made it very clear `that a hospital was badly needed—a place where the ministry of healing and the preaching of the Gospel could go hand in hand. Mr. Whipple felt they should not wait for, nor expect, all of the money for a hospital building to come from America. He felt many of the business and professional residents of Allahabad would be willing to support such a venture and he released one of the ladies to test out the people of the city for their reactions. The response was immediate. Pundit Moti Lal Nehru (father of the late Prime Minister Jawahar Lal Nehru) was one of the first to give a donation to the building which was followed by a liberal gift from Lady Maharaj Singh, wife of the Commissioner, Sir Maharaj Singh. The High Court of India is at Allahabad and the judges showed their interest in following the lead of Sir Grimwald Mears, the Chief Justice, with sizable donations. All of this was very encouraging and enabled the work of the building to commence.

Up to this time all of the buildings on the compound had been made of mud, as most of the village houses were, but Mr. Whipple felt that both for reasons of sanitation and permanence the new hospital building should be built of brick. Bricks were available in Allahabad but they were expensive and then, too, they would have to be hauled fourteen miles by ox-cart which would further add to their price. He found that the soil near the chosen building site was of the right consistency and would do very well for making brick. He found men who knew how to build a brick kiln and also how to burn the bricks and they were hired. It was a large oval-shaped kiln and as the bricks were burned and cooled, they were taken out and other unbaked ones put in their place making it a revolving self-perpetuating production. The bricks near the edge of the kiln were inferior and they were used for the inside walls while those in the center of the kiln turned out first-class, and they were used for the outside and the bearing walls.

Soon the flat field where Mr. Whipple had so often walked in the evenings praying and planning, began to take on a different look. Masons and carpenters were busy at work. At last Mr. Whipple was seeing the result of his prayers and his joy knew no bounds. Literally for very joy at the prospect of his hopes soon being fulfilled, he bounded the full length of the building site praising and thanking God for it all.

In the meantime patients continued to come for succor. A young girl was brought by her father. She had gotten too near to their camel that had become so irritable from the heat that he took her whole arm into his mouth, crushing the bone near the shoulder, then swinging her in the air until it was almost completely shredded. It was held only by a few tendons, all blood supply to the arm being cut off. When the father was told that the arm would have to be amputated, he refused permission saying, "How will I ever marry off a one-armed daughter?" They returned to their village many miles away and were never heard from again.

152

The missionaries were called to the nearby village of Hajiganj where a man had been bitten by a snake. He was already being treated by the village medicine man when they arrived, and the treatment was severe. Both ear drums had been pierced with a sharp green stick and two men, one at each side, yelled into his ear at the top of their voices to drive out the evil spirit. Buckets of cold water were poured over him to arouse him from the stupor already setting in. They were finally persuaded to allow the leg to be lanced at the site of the bite and the poison drawn off. An injection of anti-snake bite serum was given and the patient began to revive. He lived but his hearing was damaged from the drastic treatment he had received.

In the meantime while work on the hospital building was proceeding, preparations were also being made for an out-station at Bichiya, a small village about ten miles further down on the banks of the Ganges river. Kind friends had given liberally to build a small house which would accommodate two workers who could then devote their entire time to that area, preaching, teaching and healing. How the villagers flocked around when they heard that the *sahib* was coming to live among them! Daily they watched the walls of the house rise higher and higher and they gladly lent a hand to the work.

Soon the news spread into the surrounding countryside that the *sahib* who gave out the medicine at Siwait would be doing the same work here in their village. Crowds of sick and dying came to the half-built bungalow for treatment. Lest the work of building be totally interrupted, one morning of the week was set aside for treating these patients. A small shed composed of bamboos and grass mats was erected as a temporary dispensary and a nurse was brought from Siwait each week to care for these patients.

It was in the month of July and fearfully hot. Thursday, the day set for the dispensary, saw a crowd of patients assembled. As they waited Mr. Whipple who had also come out from Siwait, talked to them about their needs for healing not only for their bodies but also for their souls. He told them of the Great Healer who went about healing the sick and also breaking the power of sin, and the atonement He had provided for them. They drank in his message and then, the little meeting finished, they moved in the direction of the bamboo shed to receive their treatment.

Time is insufficient to tell of each patient, his troubles and disease. One old man with a long-standing ulcer was an object of pity. His leg was eaten away and a foul disease permeated his body. A young woman with a badly infected eyeball and lids was treated and many more. It was more than Mr. Whipple could take. He had been assisting but now he was nowhere to be seen. He was not a man who could look upon such scenes of suffering and be unmoved by them. He had quietly crept outside and there he stood behind that little bamboo shed, his face in his hands and the tears coursing down his face.

At Siwait the building of the hospital went on. A missionary nurse also arrived and a doctor had been contracted for. Mr. Whipple was able to cross off one more item on his prayer list. How grateful he was! In the days and years to come many thousands would find healing within these walls.

The inscription on front of the building expresses Mr. Whipple's sentiments:

> "We ask no other wages
> When Thou shalt call us home,
>   But to have shared the travail
> That makes Thy kingdom come."

Chapter XIII

ON THE TRAIL TO BADRINATH

"The bread that giveth life I want to give,
The water pure that bids the thirsty live,
I want to live aright from day to day;
I'm sure I shall not pass again this way."

"In the cool of the evening with shadows nigh,
  At dawn, when the sun breaks clear,
  I want the great crowd passing by,
  To ken what they see and hear.
  To glimpse the restful valleys deep,
  To toil up the rugged hill,
  To see the brooks that shyly creep,
  To have the torrents thrill.
  I want to laugh with the common man
  Wherever he chance to be,
  I want to aid him when I can
  Whenever there's need of me.
  I want to lend a helping hand
  Over the rough and steep
  To a child too young to understand—
  To comfort those who weep."

—Silas H. Perkins.

Chapter XIII

ON THE TRAIL TO BADRINATH

TEM after item was gradually being erased from the prayer list that Mr. Whipple had made nearly ten years before. The request for a house in the hills was no idle dream but a pressing need. It was hard enough to suffer the heat of the plains during the summer months but to see the babies and children suffer was the hardest of all; besides it took the missionaries from their other duties to care for sick children who would thrive and be healthy if only they were away from the heat and in the cool mountain air. Earnest prayer continued and this request was laid out before the Lord, believing that the same God who supplied the children of Israel with manna in the wilderness could supply this need also. Buying a house in the hills with their present income was out of the question yet their eyes were turned toward God, knowing full well that He was able to supply it.

Then one day there came a letter with a bank draft for ten thousand rupees—the kind gift of three persons who stated that it was for a rest home in the hills, but who modestly concealed their names. Mr. Whipple at once started "house-hunting" in Darjeeling but none of the houses for sale seemed suitable for the large mission family. Then God led his steps to Mussoorie and Landour where a large twelve-room furnished house lay vacant and procurable at the amount the missionaries were able to pay.

Hazelwood, the name of the property, was a pretty spot just off the beaten path from Landour bazaar and secluded on a steep hillside of deodars and pines. A smaller building near the entrance served as servants' quarters; while another smaller one down on the hillside was used for storage of coal and wood.

The house itself is situated on a projection of the mountain side overlooking beautiful Mussoorie and Landour bazaar. On the west lofty, fir-clad mountains rise tier on tier—first dark green, then purple, then blue, blue, blue, fading away into cloudland itself with a beautiful glimpse in the northwest of the eternal snows of Tehri and Tibet. And far below (7,000 ft.) to the south, stretching as far as eye can see, were the plains laid out like a glorious Persian carpet, decorated profusely with forests and fields and broken only by the low range of foothills known as the Siwaliks. To the right was a river winding out from among the hills. This was the Jumna, and there, to the left, clearly visible on a fine day, flowed the river sacred to a hundred million Hindus—the river Ganges. These two rivers whose sources lie in such proximity separate and follow widely different courses but are destined for each other. At Allahabad the two meet again as we have seen.

It was this beautiful situation that was designed of God to answer His children's prayers. On inquiry Mr. Whipple found that the property was in the hands of a bank whose headquarters was in Calcutta. This necessitated several trips to and from Calcutta but by the end of February (1929) the deeds and the property were in the hands of the mission and Mr. Whipple was authorized to take possession.

Mr. Whipple decided to go ahead of the crowd to make what repairs were necessary at Hazelwood, taking along a carpenter from Siwait. Landour is glorious in the springtime with a cool crispness in the air that is not unlike the spring in old New England. Perhaps it was the similarity that turned his thoughts westward over two oceans to the home of his childhood days, or perhaps it was the pine-covered hills that reminded him of the hills back home; or was it the fact that, having bought a house for the mission, he was reminded of the little cottage fancy had painted so vividly in his younger days—white with green door frame and shutters and Jessie's face always in the window? Whatever it was, he was thinking of it all as he approached Hazelwood and viewed the answer to their prayers—the *substance* of things hoped for. There it stood, a truly beautiful place all white with green woodwork and green shutters—only much larger than the dream home he had surrendered; larger for his family was larger! He had long ago forgotten the selfish "we four and no more." His family now included all who were of the family of Heaven and his children all the children of God. Silently there on the hillside he thanked God. He was glad he had exchanged his little earthly plans for Heaven's hundredfold.

But there were problems ahead. Upon entering the house they found to their surprise that not a piece of furniture was there! It was clearly stated in the contract, paid for and settled, yet it was gone—stolen, they had to assume. That was something new and unexpected, and the job of furnishing a twelve-room house with a slim purse was no small undertaking. Again Mr. Whipple went to prayer. Even the children at Siwait when they heard of it, prayed expecting God to provide for them. There were only a few days left before the children were to arrive and school begin.

In the meantime, Mr. Whipple and the carpenter worked away putting in window panes, painting, papering and installing electricity, batching as best they could with a packing case for a table, boxes for chairs, cupboards and other necessary things.

Their work went well and the place took on a trim, tidy aspect after its long vacation. But it was still void of furniture. Then one day, as Mr. Whipple chanced to glance down the hillside in the direction of the bazaar, he saw an army of coolies each with a huge pack on his back. He looked again. Yes, he was right—there was the furniture coming back as it had gone *en masse!* That called for a jubilee, for even though they had prayed it seemed incredible that it should ever be recovered. Only much fuss, a threat, or a handsome bribe could accomplish that in the East, and there it came up the hill, sent via Heaven!

As soon as the children and their teacher arrived and the house was in order, Mr. Whipple felt he should leave. His heart was in the work down on the heated plains and he felt he must be there. Bidding his family goodbye he left once more for the mission at Siwait.

With the school and the children away in the hills, much of the routine work of the missionaries was eliminated and they were set free to put more time and attention to evangelistic work in the villages.

Sixty-five different bazaars all being within a radius of twenty-five miles from the mission, Mr. Whipple felt would provide a wonderful opportunity to give out the Word of Life. These bazaars are held weekly, bi-weekly in some cases, and peasants from the most remote and insignificant villages are often among the crowd at these gatherings.

So a bazaar campaign was planned for the summer which would take in practically all of these bazaars once or twice, at least, in the course of the summer. These gatherings are usually held at two or three o'clock in the afternoon—the time when the sun's heat is at its maximum which necessitated leaving the bungalow at twelve or one o'clock and riding over hot, dusty roads with a hot wind blowing at the rate of thirty miles an hour and a temperature as high as 120 degrees in the shade.

Each of the little party was equipped with a pack of Gospels and tracts in Hindi and Urdu, the two languages common to that district. The Gospels sold at one-half cent and one cent and the tracts were distributed free to all who could read. To many of the poorer classes money is a rare commodity. Produce from their fields is often taken to the bazaar and in turn they carry home cloth, rope, or foodstuffs not grown on their own plots of land. Money does not enter into the transaction. So when the evangelist approaches a poor peasant with a Gospel selling at one cent he thinks twice before buying it. If pressed by the worker he will offer a handful of grain, some corn, or a lump of *gur* (unrefined sugar).

Often in a village bazaar of five or six hundred people, with difficulty a dozen persons could be found who could read. Mr. Whipple was always anxious not to miss one who might be a potential buyer and how often he was heard to say as they would be about to leave for home, "Oh, let me have just one more try. Maybe I can sell another one."

Mr. Whipple lived close to God and sought to improve each moment for His glory. The time spent in trips to and from these village bazaars was profitably spent. A small notebook in which he wrote difficult Hindi and Urdu words and idiomatic expressions was carried in his coat pocket and leisure moments were spent learning them. Sometimes portions of Scripture in Hindi or English were memorized or the words of a *bhajan* or English hymn. Little vest-pocket editions of the lives of famous Christians he used to carry for inspiration and encouragement.

Perhaps it was the strenuous summer work of visiting so many villages and bazaars besides attending to his editorial work and administrative affairs; or perhaps it was the long years of privation and suffering just beginning to tell on his constitution; whatever it was, Mr. Whipple felt his strength spent and, if he would be fit for the winter, he must get away for a short time. Since the rainy season had already commenced and outside meetings would have to be discontinued anyway, Mr. Whipple decided to spend a few weeks in the hills. Another separation—for Mrs. Whipple must come down and stay on at Siwait during his absence and carry on, as best she could, the work of her husband.

The monsoons had already broken when Mr. Whipple arrived in Landour and the already beautiful scenery was transformed into Elysian splendor. Ferns and flowers seemed to have dropped out of the blue. Trees were groaning under the load of ferns they bore on their trunks and branches, and large rainbow-hue dahlias, fragrant hyacinths, lilies of the valley and pink and white crocuses were everywhere.

Mr. Whipple had loved the out-of-doors from his boyhood days and as he gazed on this Himalayan wonderland of beauty the call of the wild became irresistible. For some weeks past he had gathered information of the mountainous country further north. There, nestled somewhere in those mountains, so he was told, lay Tehri, a city of about 5,000 Hindus and numerous shrines and sacred visiting places. It is situated on the banks of the turbulent Ganges where it forces its way through the lofty mountains, and about half-way to the most holy spot—Badrinath, the actual source, or one of them, of the sacred rivers where thousands of pilgrims journey every year to bathe in its sacred waters, to cook their rice in the boiling spring, and to worship at the sacred shrine of Ganga, the goddess of the Ganges.

It would be a wonderful opportunity to sow some Gospel seed and Mr. Whipple decided to go. Taking a coolie used to these parts, he would have a reliable guide, companionship, and someone to carry his load of bedding, cooking utensils, and a change of clothing. A large supply of Gospel portions, tracts and a *bhajan* book were included in his little bundle and Mr. Whipple started off expecting to be gone about ten days. Perhaps it would be best to let him tell it in his own words, extracts from letters written home to Mrs. Whipple.

Hazelwood, Landour, Musoorie,
Monday, August 26, 1929.

"My dear Jessie:

"You will not get a letter from me for a few days, maybe. I am starting this afternoon on a trip into the mountains forty miles away. There's a place called Tehri and they say the town has more than 5,000 inhabitants. I thought I could see what is there and maybe someday we could open a mission there. There is not a white person in the place. I am taking Gospels and tracts and a small *bhajan* book. I am going to take it in easy stages and cook my food on the way. I had my shoes half-soled and irons put on them. I am taking some stamps and may be able to write you just the same. I am taking a coolie, and a little tea and sugar, and will get everything else I need on the way. There are government *dak* bungalows (mail-stage bungalows) where I can stop nights. Here things are too institution-like for a rest. I want to do this kind of itinerant work next winter, only, perhaps, use a wheel, so I want to get used to it."

Dhanaulti, Dharamshala,
Tuesday, 4:30 P.M.

"Guess I will have to use pencil to save my ink. Well, here I am about fifteen miles up in the mountains. Only came about seven miles today with very little climbing. I would have gone farther but the next rest house is nine miles away and it is raining besides. All my things are nice and dry and I don't want to get them wet if I can help it. Mornings seem to be pleasanter than afternoons so I want to get a good start in the morning. It was grand all morning and the scenery was magnificent. I want to reach Tehri Thursday, but I can't say yet what I will do for sure.

"I had such a good time talking to my coolie this morning. I told him all about Christ dying, etc. and he seemed so interested. He knows Hindustani quite well; in fact, I chose a coolie who knew Hindustani as it is so hard to have one who only knows *Pahari* (language of the hill tribes). I want to read and pray with him this evening, also give out some tracts here in this place as there are several shops and *baniyas* (shopkeepers). One man has mounds and mounds of apples stored but they are too green for eating. I am thinking of buying a few and either roasting them or making some sauce.

"I have been reading a tract in Hindi entitled, *'Maut aur Zindagi'* (Death and Life) and it is the best thing I have found of its kind. I wouldn't mind buying them by the thousand and selling them in the bazaars. Its teaching against sin is so plain, and it tells how to find salvation in such a simple, common-sense style. It

Mr. and Mrs. Whipple on furlough in America.

Mr. Whipple receives a letter from his family.

has only twenty pages and there was only one word that I did not know. It has so many simple little illustrations—I wish our preachers would cultivate that style for village preaching.

"I have spent only seven annas (fourteen cents) for food so far but I had a loaf of bread, tea, sugar and jam. For dinner I made a stew of potatoes, *dal* (lentils), onions, mint—picked by the roadside—chillies, butter, salt, and water. It was real good and satisfying. My bread is about gone so I am up to making my own.

"I am wondering how it would be to have some Hindustani meetings in Landour. My coolie says he has never before heard the story of Christ.

"It is pouring rain—glad I am under shelter. There is a *dak* bungalow here but the Dharamshala (pilgrim shelter) where I am staying is fairly clean and has a very wide veranda.

"Lots of love,
"Dad".

That night Mr. Whipple listened to the patter of rain on the roof of the *dharamshala,* the thatch roof softening the sound and making it most inducive to sleep. He awoke the next morning to a bright new world, each tree and shrub freshly washed by the night's rain, and long shafts of sparkling sunlight danced on the wet pine and fir needles, and tardy rain-drops, catching the light, flashed back diamonds as transient as they were beautiful.

The path that morning started out fairly level, then became rocky and so rugged and narrow in places that

169

a misstep would mean a fall of hundreds of feet down the sheer precipice. There were places where the recent rain had caused landslips that left the mountain side scarred and dangerous for man and animals to pass. In places trees had been uprooted and dropped into deep chasms below.

In the distance the snow-capped peaks of Tibet loomed over 20,000 feet. Between here and there lay Badrinath, the place every Hindu reveres. Thousands of pilgrims risk their lives to make the hazardous pilgrimage over the snowy mountain passes which even in midsummer spawn blinding blizzards, and hundreds of pilgrims fall by the wayside and perish in the freezing cold.

Mr. Whipple saw many fellow travelers and pilgrims on the road wearing only the cotton loin cloth or sari of the plains and wondered how they would survive the cold of the high passes farther on, some over 18,000 feet. This is the road the sainted Christian Sadhu Sundar Singh trudged making his way into Tibet to preach the Gospel. A Tibetan he chanced to meet was his fellow-traveler. As they arrived up in the high mountain passes they encountered a blizzard and struggled against the blinding snow and wind trying to make the next town before darkness overtook them. Suddenly they heard groans and crying. Someone had fallen over the precipice. The Sadhu stopped and asked his Tibetan companion to clamber down the mountainside with him to help the poor unfortunate man. He refused saying they would never make the town by nightfall and a night out in this blizzard would mean certain death. The Sadhu replied, "But I am a

Christian and my religion teaches me to help my neighbor," and down the precipice he climbed to lend succor. The Tibetan shook his head and continued on his journey.

The Sadhu helped the fallen man up and, wrapping his shawl around the two of them and bracing himself against the storm, slowly and laboriously made their way into town. Dawn was just breaking as they neared their goal and they looked down by the roadside, where a figure lay frozen in the snow. It was his Tibetan companion of the night before. Mr. Whipple often used this incident in his talks. "He that saveth his life shall lose it; and he that loseth his life for My sake and the Gospel shall find it."

Again the next evening he writes:

Kandia, 28 miles
from Musoorie,
Wednesday eve.

"My dear Jessie:

"The heading will let you know where I am. I want to make Tehri tomorrow. Expect to come back here by next Sunday as it is a beautiful place. There is a little forest bungalow here with a nice green lawn, the yard and paths all bordered with sunflowers. It is so clean and such a relief from the coolie *dharamshalas* —will have a bed for the first time since Sunday. It is such a beautiful spot, overshadowed by pine-covered mountains. The houses along the road are very scarce—this is the first house on the road for about five miles. There are little villages in the valleys.

"I had a good clean-up tonight after I cooked my food. I made *gili kicheri* and *bunjia* (or nearer stew of potatoes, onions, chillies and *ghi* (clarified butter), *chappatis*, plum jam and tea. Not a bad camp meal.

"Have had a chance to sell some Gospels and give out some tracts along the way. Have also talked much to my coolie along salvation lines and sang and explained '*Raja Yisu Aya*' (King Jesus has come) to a party in the *dharamshala* this morning. Had a fine time praying—feel the native work on me very strong.

"My coolie says I will get rid of all my Gospels in Tehri. I haven't a great pack left but enough to lead one person into the light if they fall into the hands of some hungry souls. I don't know where I will mail this—probably in Tehri tomorrow. There is no Post Office in this place. Well, I must write a few lines to the four.

"Lots of love,
"Dad."

And the following day he wrote:

Tehri

"My dear Jessie:

"Well here I am at last. I got here about four o'clock yesterday. This place is just forty miles from Mussoorie. It is a beautiful little place—makes me think of old Mystic as it used to be—no telephones, nor

172

telegraph, no lights nor railway—so quiet and sleep-like.

"Tehri is only about 3,000 feet above sea level. The last fifteen miles was all down hill so that means it will be all up going home—no, the first three miles will be level and then up for twelve miles. Some of the places along the way are higher than Landour (7,500 feet). This place is much warmer than Mussoorie. There is a beautiful breeze here in the *Dak bungalow*. It is right above where the Ganges comes tearing along. Tehri is built at the head of a little valley where two mountains meet, there being just enough space to let the river through. The river flows between rather high cliffs and the Raja has his palace right across the river from the *dak* bungalow on a cliff about 300 feet high. It is beautiful here with the river in front and the mountains on all sides.

"I was very much surprised last night by the visit of a very fair man dressed with a plaid kilt, a yellow turban, blue leggings, bare-footed, long curly hair and a *lohi* thrown around him. He is out on his own to study up on the Hindu religion. He lives on one meal a day, nearly all raw stuff. When he asked who I was, I mentioned the *Burning Bush*. He stretched out his hand to me at once and said, 'I like that paper. My mother sends me some once in a while.' He brought me a big dish of a sort of fruit salad for breakfast—apples and melons cut up together, and tonight he is bringing me my dinner and told me not to cook anything. My coolie (who lives near here) went home last night. He has been away since March. As we came we passed within a mile of his home, and as I had some field glass-

173

es, I let him take a look at his house. He got a surprise and kept saying, 'This makes my house close by.' He even recognized his father in front of the house. So many of the folks around here go to Mussoorie for the summer to work. Many of them know Hindi and if we had a place in Landour bazaar, we no doubt, could get many of them in for meetings.

"Had a good time praying today. I believe the Lord is going to show us how we can make our work most effective for Him. I feel like praying, 'Lord, send forth the laborers.'

"I gave the letters I wrote at Kandia to some men going to Mussoorie with instructions to mail them there. I am feeling fine. The fresh air and sunshine are a fine tonic. Down this side the rains are over for the season.

"Love,
"Dad."

Mr. Whipple arrived back in Mussoorie the following Wednesday and work awaited him. Stacks of letters lay awaiting replies, arrangements for workers had to be made and he was able to throw himself into the work again, refreshed and encouraged.

Chapter XIV

DRUM-BEAT AT THE VILLAGE SHRINE

"I have only one candle of life to burn and I would rather burn it out in a land of darkness than in a land flooded with light."

—Anon.

Sikandra Shrine

"Shall we, who souls are lighted
        With wisdom from on high—
Shall we to men benighted,
        The lamp of life deny?
Salvation! Oh, salvation!
        The joyful sound proclaim,
Till earth's remotest nation
        Has learned Messiah's name."

                    —*Reginald Heber.*

176

Chapter XIV

DRUM-BEAT AT THE
VILLAGE SHRINE

HE long India summer was drawing to a close. The air which in the early part of the summer had been parchingly dry, then later, in the rainy season, humid and sultry, was now once again cool and balmy making one feel that it was meant to breathe and live in.

With the coming of the winter season, new activities were being planned for the spread of the Gospel and the enlargement of the work. Mr. Whipple had long desired to pioneer new villages in more distant parts. He wanted even closer contact with the villager in order to better understand his thinking and to reach him with the Christian message.

The district of Sikandra had long attracted the attention of the missionaries. It was teeming with people many of whom had never once heard the name of Jesus. To this district around Sikandra Mr. Whipple decided to go. Leaving much of his work at Siwait to his faithful wife, from whom he had already been parted nearly the whole of the summer, he prepared for a new campaign of toil and sacrifice for the salvation of these people he had learned to love more dearly than life itself.

The party consisted of four—two Indian workers and two missionaries. A tent was taken along to serve as a headquarters and supply station; four cycles on which to ride to the surrounding villages; solar *topis*; flasks of boiled water to strap to their backs while cycling as a safeguard against contaminated water; some food which could not be procured so far afield; and Mata Din, the servant to watch the tent and carry supplies and mail to and from Siwait. And the party was off.

Most of the luggage was carried by ox-cart early in the day, and late in the afternoon the party of four arrived on cycles. Crowds of villagers flocked to the grove as soon as it was noised about that the missionaries had arrived. Hastily things were unpacked and the tent laid out but it was already getting dark before it could be erected. Daylight fades into darkness so quickly in the tropics that twilight is unknown.

Just after the tent had been put up and they were settling in, a call came from a nearby village. A woman was ill, desperately ill, and unless medical help could be obtained she probably would not live the night through. To find a doctor who would go to such an out-of-the-way place at that time of night was out of the question and the nearest nurse was in Allahabad twenty-five miles away! But her life was in danger and much of the success of their winter's work depended on how they would act now.

The motor car from Siwait was procured and Mrs. Whipple went to Allahabad to get a nurse. It was late when they reached Allahabad and nearly midnight before motor, nurse and Mrs. Whipple arrived back in the grove at Sikandra where the tent had been pitched, to get a guide to take them to the patient's house. Mata

Din had made a fire and had a kettle boiling which reminded Mrs. Whipple that she had had no supper. Hastily taking some bread and butter and a hot cup of tea, they proceeded on to the village a few miles farther to where the sick woman lay.

The night was still save for the occasional bark of a village dog and the distant howl of hungry jackals. The air was crisp and the stars were one by one slowly setting in the west.

The house to which they were directed was a mud-walled structure with low, heavy beams overlaid with grass and topped with tile for a roof. The patient lay on the mud floor obviously in great pain. The nurse examined her and she did what she could to relieve her pain to no avail. She would get relief only if she could be taken to a hospital and be operated on, but this the husband refused to allow. How earnestly they pleaded until the early hours of the morning but no, the husband was adamant. "Jo ho, so ho. Ham kya kare?" was his attitude—whatever will be, will be; what can we do? "We will wait until tomorrow and see what happens," they said, so Mrs. Whipple and the nurse went back to the camp sad, and tired and dejected.

The first faint streaks of light could just be seen in the east so rather than awaken Mr. Whipple and the others who had also been up very late the night before, they strolled over to a nearby grove. As the sun rose its golden rays shone on the village of Sikandra where hundreds of temples and shrines with their domes and minarets, were silhouetted against the sky. They drew near to one of the temples and examined its grotesque idols. There sat Mahadeo, the god of water, bedaubed with red paint and garlands of marigolds. Bits of broken clay dishes were the only remains of the faithful, howbeit misled, devotees' recent offerings.

Sikandra is the home of many staunch Hindus. In this one village alone there are 365 Hindu temples so that one might worship at a different shrine every day of the year and not leave his native village. Just outside the village in a shady grove is a shrine surrounded by a high mud wall where a *mela* is held every Sunday. Within those walls is a Mohammedan tomb where years ago a well-known, beneficent Mohammedan landowner was buried. Here week by week hundreds of Hindu villagers come to perform their *pujas* and, at the same time, visit their friends and join in the sports attendant on all such occasions.

The elderly and more devout of the Hindus present may be seen around the wall of the enclosure, standing on one foot with face against the wall, beating their bodies as they pray. Small clay dishes of oil, handfuls of meal, or a few marigold blossoms are brought as an offering to the god within the temple which they know as Gaja Mia.

Mr. Whipple yearned over these sad sights and his heart burned within him. Daily he went about teaching the people as his lowly Master had done so many years before him, and sought to bring them to the knowledge of the better way.

The following letter was written to Mrs. Whipple from Sikandra:

Ready for a day in the villages: from left; Tyrrell Fordham, Stephen de la Place, Mr. Whipple, and Herbert Hyratt.

Whipple Family: John, Norman, Jessie, Alice, Marjorie, and Earle.

"My dear Jessie:

"Just a line to go with Mata Din. We are all out this morning—at least, three of us, Herbert is cooking today, I tomorrow, Tyrrell Wednesday and Thursday. I cooked breakfast yesterday morning and had hot boiled potatoes, brown goat stew, spinach (really a weed), cucumber salad, apricots, bread, butter and tea. Everything came out quite decent.

"It is fine to work this way. We may go together for meetings after we have paved the way. A Brahmin from Sikandra came in last night and had a talk.

"We drew cuts as to what direction to go. Herbert goes toward home; Tyrrell towards the Ganges; Stephen towards Partabgarh, and I have the east. We do not have to go far from the main road to find densely populated districts. I only worked two villages this morning—the folks came crowding around so that I couldn't get away. I found a man who had been to our hospital with his child who had a bad ear and it got well. He was so very friendly.

"We are having our morning prayers in Hindustani and then will have prayers together in English as we have opportunity. I am going to take a little food with me for noon and stay out all day as it takes so much time and strength going back and forth. I will plan on having a good, substantial breakfast before going out and a good dinner in the evening. I think we will all prefer this way of doing. I am staying in this afternoon as Mata Din is using my cycle and I had some writing to do.

"Now for the things we need. Some money. Milk is ten annas a day. We buy meat and can get eggs, rice and *dal* here; we also can get coal but it is rather expensive, so you can please bring some when you come. Also send some vegetables. We ought to have these things as soon as convenient for you.

"Please get our knapsacks soon as it is so hot we do not wear a coat and have no good pockets in our trousers. We ought to have a tube of tire-mending rubber cement each for our bicycles and enough patches for four mending kits. I feel God's blessing on me. It certainly is a privilege to be able to do this work. I am praying especially for some Indian young men to get salvation and give their lives for this work.

"I was a little disappointed not seeing you yesterday. I am praying for you.

"Lots of love,
"Dad"

Again he writes:

"My dear Jessie:

"As Brother Fordham is going tomorrow to get his bike fixed up, I thought you would like a letter.

"There is not much news except that I am working as much as possible. I had a good afternoon though the morning went hard. Found a little girl today who, I am sure, was starting with leprosy there. She had a white spot with a red center on her nose and her father was greatly agitated about her, an innocent-looking thing

183

to cause such havoc. They were *chamars* and the father promised to take her to the hospital.

"I want a little wooden box with a cover that I can lock, or wire to my cycle carrier so I can take some *dawai* (medicine) with me. A few simple remedies do open up the way like everything.

"Am planning on working nearby places tomorrow morning, then I want to visit a bazaar in my territory with books in the afternoon, I find some hopeful cases. I am going to some villages the second time and nearly everybody is very friendly.

"Surely the fields are white and the laborers are few. I am praying that the Lord will make me a blessing in this country. I don't know whether it means to live or die—the Lord knows—but I feel like pouring out my life and believe God will bless the sacrifice.

"Lots of love,
"Dad."

Many books and Gospels were scattered in that district and one bright little Brahmin boy bought a Gospel according to St. Matthew. A few months passed by and then someone chanced to visit the home where the family of this boy lived. It was the mother who came out to greet the missionary and who told them of her son who had died in the meantime. Then she brought out a little well-thumbed Gospel of St. Matthew. "This is what he loved to read," she said, as she showed it to the worker. Special verses had been underlined and read and reread. The missionary wanted to take the little booklet home but the mother would not part with it. "It meant so much to my son and was his constant companion before he died. I cannot part with it now." So saying that sorrowful Brahmin mother went indoors again after carefully wrapping her son's treasure in a small square of red cloth.

All through that last winter spent at Sikandra Mr. Whipple carried an intense burden for souls. Perhaps he realized or had a premonition that his time for labor was short. He memorized the words of the hymn, "Work for the night is coming" and often during those last few months he was heard singing that hymn.

The long days were spent in going from village to village and talking with the people, healing what of their sores and troubles he could, and proclaiming the Gospel of a living Savior waiting to pardon their sins. Arriving back at the tent, sometimes long after dark, he ate his supper but even then he did not consider his day's work done. Wandering off to a nearby grove he would pour out his soul in prayer to God. He realized it is not by might nor by one's own power but that it must be by the Holy Spirit if these souls should come to know the true God. While all else around was still, save for the occasional bark of a village dog or the call of the village *chaukidar* (watchman) on his hourly beat, his low voice could still be heard pouring out his petitions to his Heavenly Father.

The village work came to a halt for ten days during which the annual Camp Meeting was held in Allahabad. This series of meetings was held yearly in

185

January chiefly for the benefit of the English-speaking people of that city and those from other parts of India who could attend. Many heard the call of God as the faithful preacher sounded forth the demands of the Gospel night after night, and a few, thank God, surrendered to Him. The last day of the meetings Mr. Whipple was ill and confined to his bed all day. While he lay there the Holy Spirit flashed a message on his mind for the evening service: "The harvest is past, the summer is ended, and we are not saved." Ill though he was, his thought was not of himself or his own bodily weakness. Before the service he arose and dressed and went to preach before that crowded tent, weak in body but strong in the power of the Spirit. Never had his words carried such weight and none who attended that meeting will soon forget the message. During the course of that sermon he mentioned that it might be the last time he would ever stand before them. It was.

An urgent call, like a Macedonian cry, had long been coming from the southland. Mr. Whipple considered this interval between the meetings and his village work an opportune time to make his long-promised visit. The spiritual awakening in the Malayalam district in the south had its origin in the time of the apostles. We are told that after Pentecost St. Thomas came to South India and through his ministry many of these South Indian people were converted to Christianity. Today they are a people Christian in name but, in many villages, still half pagan, groping blindly for the true light. Mr. Whipple's constant prayer was for more laborers to send into these needy areas.

Everywhere people were calling for help but where were the Spirit-filled workers to send?

Most of Mr. Whipple's trip will have to be from his own words gathered from the following letters which speak for themselves.

Madras Station
Friday, January 24, 1930

"My dear Jessie:

"As I have all day here I will have a chance to do some letter writing. We leave here at nine o'clock tonight and then ride about 500 miles from here arriving Sunday 3 a.m. so the train must be a very slow one. I think we go through without a change. Mr. A. is my host on this trip, also my banker, so I have no worries.

"Unless I have special business in Calcutta I am thinking of booking by the other route on the return journey (via Nagpur). I have a rather strong urge to stop off and see G.T. This would be a little out of my way but not too much and I might be able to do him some good.

"This is the first time I have been in Madras since passing through on my way to America. This trip revives memories of that time but they are not altogether pleasant ones. I am glad I am not on the same errand this time, leaving wife and children behind in India!

"We had a good rest last night—each of us had a bench to himself and we were disturbed very little. The way I lay made my side ache and it still feels a little tired. I also had a headache this morning but that has passed off."

Sunday night,
Kotarakara

"Dear Jessie:

"I hardly know where to begin; I tried to get a letter off to you yesterday but the train stopped such a little time at the different stations and shook so that I could not write while traveling.

"I wrote you last from Madras—well, we left Madras at nine Friday evening and rode all that night and all day yesterday. We got to our destination about four this morning, but to make it interesting the coach we were in did not go through, so about 11:30 we had to get up and out of the train, and then to add to the fun we only had sitting up room in the carriage we got into. That meant very little sleep until we got in the station about four o'clock this morning. The floor of the waiting room did feel good and no mistake.

"After cleaning up (and we needed it, as we had on the same clothes that we started with) we went to Mr. M's place about nine this morning. We found him gone and Thomas also. A boy there could talk a little English, so he was our interpreter. The women all know nothing but Malayalam. Mr. A. wanted me to visit a boy who is attending school about fifty miles away, and as we could do nothing here, I suggested that we go

188

over today. Mr. A. was agreed and we started. We went by bus and I must say that I enjoyed the trip. The air was about like a nice day at home (America) in early May. The country is rolling with cocoanut palms, banana trees and bamboos in abundance. The country right around here is quite hilly and coming up on the train we passed through the longest tunnel I have seen in India.

"The people here are different from those I have met anywhere else. Some of the women wear nothing at all on the upper part of their bodies but those belong to the lower classes. There are many Christians and there are a few temples and many churches. The people on the whole are rather attractive and intelligent looking. We met Mr. M. here when we came home.

"I am planning on staying here this week anyway unless I get an urgent wire. I may start for home next week, about the middle, break journey over Sunday at G.T's and get home about Tuesday. That would make it about two weeks from the day after tomorrow, about the twelfth of next month. Is that too long? I am praying to be a blessing wherever I go.

"Mr. M. says that he is going to get a place for us in Kotarakara that will be handier for us than this. Of course, the language problem is a hard one. If we could get young men to get some training at Siwait and when they return home, a work might be done as they seem very susceptible to the Gospel. It is different from working among raw heathen. But we will just pray and let God lead.

"I trust that Miss Workman and party are blessed in working among the *mela* crowds. I feel such a burden for the people around Siwait."

Karickan,
Kotarakara
Monday

"My dear Jessie:

"We got back here this afternoon. I found that your letter had arrived and while the news was rather stale I enjoyed it so much and have read it over three or four times. I think I will have no trouble in carrying out my schedule.

"There are a lot of missions in this section. I imagine that it is easier to get a crowd here than in the north, but I do not know about getting people to die to self—whether it would be easier or not. Dying is not much sought after naturally by any class of people. I wouldn't be surprised if it would not be possible to do something in this section if we only had the right kind of workers.

"The young man whom we went to see, knows English quite well. We have been talking to him and may be able to get a hook in his jaw. He is only eighteen and personally I've much more faith for a young person, though, of course, God can help anybody.

"We are living rather rough. Thursday evening we did not have dinner until eleven at night, and rice and prawn curry at that. We have three meetings booked for Sunday—two in one place and one in the other. Where I have been having meetings there were about seventy-five or a hundred, I think, at least the room was crowded.

"I wanted to write Bud a birthday letter but I have been so busy that I did not get around to it. I could have done it if I had thought of it in time."

"With love to the five,
"Dad"

"In the woods,
I don't know where,
Saturday A.M.

"Dear Jessie:

"There was a little company of people that Mr. A. wanted me to visit. We had a meeting last night and both of us spoke through an interpreter. I am getting a little used to it now, but would not care to preach that way all the time. Did not finish meeting until after eleven. They start late here and then with an interpreter the meeting takes longer. Then about eleven-thirty or later, we sat down to a rice and chicken curry dinner. How's that? But I do not feel badly though I will probably get sleepy later on. We will return home by bus today in time for meeting there.

"When we came here we stopped a few minutes to rest at the young man's house that I spoke about. While

191

we were waiting one boy ran off and came back shortly afterwards with about twelve or fifteen freshly-picked bananas; another climbed a tree and got us each a green cocoanut. He broke open one end and gave it to us to drink. They are full of water when young, then they gradually thicken until they become hard. The water is rather cooling and nice.

"This place is away up in the woods on a rocky hill. We stayed in a schoolhouse that belongs to the people. They have recently built a sort of tabernacle that will hold more than 5,000 people for conventions. They try to make it comfortable for us and are very hospitable.

"This is really a beautiful country—a great deal like some of New England hills and valleys and ledges. There are houses built all over the hills and in the valleys.

"I feel the fire of God burning bright and clear. I believe God is going to help us in our work for Him."

"Yours with love,
"Dad"

Mr. Whipple returned to Siwait about the middle of February and the next few weeks were busy ones. He was compelled to sit at his desk for hours at a time answering the letters which had accumulated during his absence.

One morning as he sat thus engaged, a tall, bearded Mohammedan stepped into his office, worried and troubled. Mr. Whipple glanced up from his letters to see a familiar face. It was Shabbar Hosain for whom he had prayed all these years. Jumping up from his

192

chair, he extended his hand to him and asked him to sit down. Then Shabbar Hosain told his story; he had already lost one child and two more were ill at home. Would someone go and see them? Mr. Whipple consented to send help and Shabbar Hosain rose and departed. What the disease would prove to be Mr. Whipple did not know but not for a moment would he hesitate to help his brother in need. He had prayed for this man too long, now by one selfish act, to stand in the way, perhaps, of his finding Christ.

The next two weeks passed as so many weeks and months, yes, years, had passed—in editing the *Burning Bush* copy and writing for it; overseeing the farm, carpenters and masons; then weary and tired, preaching in the villages at night. Yet even in those days of routine and toil his soul seemed to have caught the vision of the City Celestial. His thoughts, his conversations, and his sermons were of Heaven and one could not be in his presence without feeling something of his godly influence. Even then during those busy days God above—unknown to any mortal being—was preparing for him a "far more exceeding and eternal weight of glory."

Chapter XV

TWILIGHT AND EVENING BELL

*"I declare, now that I am dying, that I would not
have spent my life otherwise for the whole world."*

—David Brainerd

Hazelwood,
Landour, Mussoorie,

"*Abide with me; fast falls the eventide,*
The darkness deepens; Lord, with me abide;
When other helpers fail and comforts flee,
Help of the helpless, O abide with me.

I fear no foe, with Thee at hand to bless;
Ills have no weight, and tears no bitterness.
Where is death's sting? where, grave, thy victory?
I triumph still, if thou abide with me."

                              —Henry F. Lyte.

Chapter XV

TWILIGHT AND EVENING BELL

T was late April and the heat on the plains had already been intense for many weeks. It became evident to all that they should get the children away to the hills. It was decided that Mrs. Whipple and the teacher should take the children while Mr. Whipple was to remain on the plains at Siwait.

Preparations had all been made and Mrs. Whipple had planned to leave very early Wednesday morning. At the last moment certain urgent business at Hazelwood made it necessary for Mr. Whipple to accompany them. As he stepped into the car to go to the station he passed the remark that he only intended to be gone for the weekend and that he hoped to return to Siwait the following Monday.

Little did those of the mission band who had gathered around the car that April morning to bid their friends Godspeed realize that that was the last goodbye they would give their leader. They thought they were farewelling him to the hills for a few days; little did they dream this would be his final farewell.

The trip had been planned by way of Fyzabad instead of via Partabgarh, the usual route. It would be longer but occasion one less change of trains which would be trying at best with so many little ones. The

197

train was very crowded, especially the third class compartments in which the party was to travel. There were lovely first and second class compartments but they were reserved for those who could pay more, not for those who confessed that they were strangers and pilgrims on this earth. True, they could have used the money that had come from America and have traveled with more comfort, but then would this not stint the poor around them and "hinder the Gospel of Christ"? With that true missionary spirit they endured these little privations and counted it a joy to suffer a little for the sake of the One who had suffered so much for them.

The only third class compartment available was a zenana where the men are not permitted to enter, so into this the ladies and children went while Mr. Whipple went into another which already was filled to its capacity.

One must see a zenana to rightly appreciate this journey. Crowded with chattering women, noisy children, crying babies, boxes, bundles, bedding rolls, cooking utensils, kerosene cans, *surahis* of drinking water and various other household effects, some on shelves, some under the benches, in the aisles, jammed up against the carriage doors and even suspended from hooks in the ceiling. The traveler, if unable to find a seat on one of the long benches, must squat on his box or roll of bedding and get along as best he can.

In Lucknow they had a short wait. It was just after sunset and the sky was lit up with those delicate tints so peculiar to the tropics. There in the rosy-tinted light of that sunset hour they gazed out over the city, once the scene of siege and turmoil, where "Moslim mosque and pagan shrine" still raise their silver domes against the sky.

It was watermelon season and Mr. Whipple found some nice red ones that promised to be sweet and juicy. They almost looked as nice as the ones he used to love as a boy back in old New England. He bargained with the fruit seller for enough for the group and then made his way back to the train to treat the party.

When morning came their train was just pulling into Dehra Dun, the railway terminus. From here the journey must be by motor to Rajpur, a distance of seven miles. In those days there was no motor road to Mussoorie and Landour, and the only mode of travel for the remainder of the trip was by *dandies,* boat-like chairs carried on the shoulders of four coolies, or by pony, or on foot. The small children were carried in baskets on coolies' backs, the ladies rode in dandies while Mr. Whipple rode a horse.

It was midmorning and the sun's rays were hot and piercing. The road was steep and the first half of the climb lay through rocky, treeless mountains. Mr. Whipple was already ill and unfit for travel. He began to feel faint, his head was paining severely and a cruel ague shook his frame. Was it fever? He thought it was, and of no ordinary kind. He knew he was desperately ill.

He thought of dismounting and resting until the others would catch up with him, but the thought of the cooler air up higher urged him on. He would feel better then, he thought. He went a few miles farther but he could ride no more. Dismounting, he staggered to the side of the road and dropped down in a shady spot by the roadside.

It was some little time before the party reached the place where he lay only half-conscious of what was going on around him. Mrs. Whipple soon sensed the situation and, giving orders to the coolies, had him carried in her dandy the rest of the journey.

Hazelwood has always been generous, and when her capacity has apparently been reached she can always welcome another guest. The party that arrived the twenty-sixth of April met the same cordial welcome and soon felt at home. The air was crisp and cool and the sun shone bright and clear. The mountains were gorgeous in the sparkling sunlight. Mr. Whipple had always loved those hills with their deodar and pine, but he seemed not to notice anything that day. He only wanted to rest so went straight to his room.

Could it be—Mrs. Whipple was thinking long, long thoughts—that one of those insidious tropical fevers had seized him in its venomous grip? Best to play safe, she thought, so the servants' quarters on the side of the hill were made as comfortable as could be done hurriedly.

It was a pretty spot on a projection of the hillside over-looking gay Mussoorie and the Chakrata hills; to the north, snowcapped peaks reared their heads behind range after range of blue-gray mountains; below, just below in the valley rises a hillock with all the natural beauty and splendor of Scottish Abbey Craig, but it goes unnamed and unnoticed, lost amid the more imposing peaks of the grand Himalayas; down, far down, lay the sun-baked plains. How good is God! Mr.

Whipple might have been lying down on the plains somewhere in that awful heat with a burning fever. In the cool climate he should soon regain his strength.

And could it be—Mr. Whipple was also thinking some long thoughts—could it be that he had contracted that worst of all diseases, smallpox? He remembered Shabbar Hosain, his visit and his sorrowful plea for his children ill with smallpox, and the handshake—ah, that was it! But he had done it for his Lord. He had hoped and prayed for Shabbar Hosain's salvation for those many years. Perhaps through this act of kindness and affection his prayer would yet be answered.

Day by day he lay, his body aching with cruel pain, but his thoughts were not of himself. Down there, away down there on the plains lay village after village where a Gospel message has never yet been heard and from his sick bed he could see the smoke of their home-fires ascending, where thousands more know suffering keener than his, and no comfort in Christ. And how he prayed and pleaded with God on their behalf! Then he thought of Siwait the scene of so many years of arduous labor—and he prayed, prayed far into the night and all of his waking moments, that God would send the light and bring many to know his Lord.

Mrs. Whipple watched by that bedside anxiously, prayerfully, tenderly, anticipating each little want and necessity even before he was aware of them. But even love, bound though it be with the strongest ties, cannot forever hold its own. A gift, a loan just for a day, and the dearest ties must be broken. To Mrs. Whipple it became more and more evident that God was preparing to take him to Himself. She could part with him, but the work! Who will carry on his work? Would the workers and other missionaries care for those souls as he had done? God who doeth all things well would care for them. "He buries His workmen but carries on His work." Even then while these thoughts were filling her mind the angel host above were preparing to bear the earth-worn toiler to his eternal rest.

Early on Sunday morning ere the darkness of that last, long night had vanished, he called his wife to his bedside and spoke a few parting words. He bade her tell the children goodbye—the "four" as he often called them. She spoke of Heaven and the shortness of their coming separation. "You are just going a little before us. It won't be long." How sacred is the brink of the grave! Mr. Whipple knew no more. For several hours they watched by his side as life slowly ebbed away. It was just nine-thirty, the hour of his usual Sunday morning service, but he was not there. The little flock met as they were accustomed to do but their pastor had joined the church triumphant in that other City.

It was Mrs. Whipple herself who conveyed the sad tidings to the now fatherless children in the bungalow above, and the others who had loved him so dearly. The day wore on and dark black clouds announced a heavy thunder shower which broke with all the violence of a summer thunderstorm. It seemed Heaven too would hide her face from such a scene as earth had just witnessed. Unconsciously one's mind went back to that other day when Heaven hid her face from Calvary.

Then, as on that other day, the storm subsided. Where clouds had been just a few moments before, the sky was radiant with sunshine; it was blue, blue, never had it seemed so blue before. Bright-winged Himalayan songbirds warbled until the hillsides resounded with their song. Can it be that Heaven whispers her secrets and shares her joys with these and, while seraph throngs above welcome a conqueror home, these winged-creatures of earth echo back their refrain?

In the afternoon a bent, aged form was seen entering the Hazelwood gateway. News of Mr. Whipple's illness had spread and, in spite of the infectious nature of the disease, this aged fellow-missionary had come to visit him and, if possible, to relieve his suffering and minister comfort. Dr. Lucas was endeavoring to pass the thorny barrier put there to obstruct incautious intruders, when someone accosted him. Mr. Whipple had gone, they told him, and was even now in his Father's presence above. The old veteran missionary turned his steps away from the gateway, not forgetting to leave a message of comfort for the grieving hearts there. Dr. Lucas proved to be God's messenger. His taking over the burden of all arrangements for burial was a great relief and help, as no one from Hazelwood dared leave the premises lest the fearful infection be carried to others.

About six that evening a plain white casket was borne on the shoulders of six dusky men in khaki up the pathway from the hillside below. As it passed the bungalow loving hands were ready with flowers which they laid upon it as it passed by. This was their last token of affection for the one who had meant so much to them. To some he had been a father, to others a pastor and leader, and silently they brushed away the tears that came unsought. They could follow only as far as the gateway and there stood as the casket was borne up the hillside, around the bend and then disappeared out of their sight.

The sun had already set when the cemetery was reached. Dark, purple shadows filled the valleys while the last sunset hues rested on the higher peaks and lit with a soft, fading light the snow-clad mountains beyond. A few friends had gathered, among them a fellow-missionary, Dr. Elizabeth Taylor, who always seemed to know when her presence was needed at a sick bed, in time of sorrow and grief, or there was a situation of hunger and need. Kind thoughtful hands had lined the grave with clusters of daisies, and large Marechal Niel roses sent forth a fragrance that bespoke the influence of his godly life. Softly and sweetly over the evening air came the song:

> "Some day when fades the golden sun
> Beneath the rosy tinted west,
> My blessed Lord will say, 'Well done!'
> And I shall enter into rest.
> And I shall see Him face to face,
> And tell the story saved by grace."

The last strains had not died away when our minds went back to the days when Mr. Whipple used to sing that song. Especially during that last summer had his mind dwelt on Heaven's reality and often on summer evenings when returning from a village meeting, tired and exhausted from the day's strenuous labors, he would sing that song. His eyes would fill with tears as he sang:

"Some day my earthly house will fall;
 I cannot tell how soon 'twill be,
But this I know, my All-in-all
 Has now a place in Heaven for me."

His frail bark had weathered many a storm. At last it had found a haven in the City Eternal.

AFTERGLOW

"After the night of darkness,
  The shadows all flee away;
After the day of sadness,
  Hope sheds her brightest ray;
After the strife and struggle,
  The victory is won;
After the work is over,
  The Master's own word, 'Well done!' "

"The day dies slowly in the western sky;
    The sunset splendor fades, and wan and cold
The far peaks wait the sunrise; cheerily
    The goatherd calls the wanderers to their fold.

And springtime sings in deodar and pine
    Through golden hours, but all the joys they bring
Must pass thee by, no longer thine,
    For thou art where far fairer voices sing.
But we remember and ofttimes will stray
    Where rests thy form on India's lone hillside,
And softly whisper, e'er we turn away,
    Our vow to labor and in faith abide.

Be still, my soul; thine hour shall also come,
    When along the path of prayer thou wilt reach
                                    thy home."

                                —J. F. Randall.

208

AFTERGLOW

"Under the stars he sleeps, but his spirit is waking;
Low lies the grave of the man who died for his vision,
Died for the truth that he loved and the dream of his duty,
For his compassion for men and his love for Jehovah."

Under the stars he sleeps; no more will Mr. Whipple's voice be heard in India's groves agonizing in prayer over a lost world—no more from his lips will be heard in villages, town and city those stirring, Spirit-filled messages calling the prodigal home to his Savior. His work is done and that part of the great plan of redemption that was his is finished.

Yet today in India in the quiet hours of early dawn may still be heard the call of the muezzin as he summons the devotees of Allah to prayer; still, in spite of the lives laid down in their behalf, millions of devout Hindus perform their long hot dusty pilgrimages to the banks of the Ganges in search of peace, bow down before pagan shrines, and offer from their penury something with which to appease the gods; and worshipful Parsees still sprinkle out over the waters at eventide the holy fire and make oblations to the three sacred elements; and pious Jains still sit in their cross-legged fashion and read from their sacred Agamas in search of truth; and far to the north, beyond the Himalayas, the lands of Nepal, Bhutan and Tibet still present to the missionary a tremendous challenge—Tibet—a country three times the size of France where over a hundred million Tibetans waft their prayer flags to the breeze and twirl their prayer wheels. And

"Still at the end of the way lies Lhasa the Sacred,
Lhasa whose pain still knows no touch of the Healer,
Lhasa whose sin still knows no hope of Redeemer."

We speak of India and her immediate neighbors—
what shall we say of the lands of Africa, China, South
America and the islands of the sea? It is not enough
that missionaries' bones bleach in nearly every clime;
that the great missionary explorer plunged into the
heart of Africa and paid for it with his life; that Indians
in the heart of Ecuador murdered their would-be bene-
factors; that in distant Burma the Hopia tree stands
over a lonely grave; that on that Himalayan mountainside Mr. Whipple laid down his life in the cause he so
loved; yes, and there down on the heated plains there
lies another even more recent grave with the sod scarce
heaped upon it? It is not enough—until the cross of
Christ is planted in every land our cry must be, "We will
give them the Gospel or die in the attempt!"

> "In heathen lands the grasses grow
> On lofty grave mounds, row on row,
>   That mark their place; and 'bove the sky
>   The angel hosts adoring vie
> With those who greater glory know.
>
> But are they dead? our hearts may ask;
> They lived, performed their glorious task,
> Spent and were spent, and now they bask
>   In Gloryland.
>
> Fill up the ranks depleted so!
> To us from failing hands they throw
>   The torch; be ours to hold it high.
>   If we break faith with those who die,
> On us the shame! For grasses grow
>   In heathen lands."

IN MEMORY

IN MEMORY

There is the office to where he would go when his hard
days's work was done;
There is the well where he stood a while, e'er sank the
glowing sun:
The mango trees in their calm, proud strength are seen
through the purple haze,
And there Sarpat Lane wherein he walked in the
evenings of summer days;
There is the desk in the office, where his papers he
used to keep;
But our dear leader himself is gone—he's taking a quiet
sleep.

Siwait is lonely without his smile and the place has a
different look;
There is something wanting to make it nice, like the
loss of a treasured book.
The kindly face with the soft gray eyes, and the cheery
voice is gone
With the loving grasp of the gentle hand,—all make the
heart feel lone.

And didn't he toil? From early morn till daylight shut
her eyes,
There was rarely a pause for his working hands, no
time for idle sighs.
Now the paper has lost his busy brain, the printshop
lost his form;
He has woven the web of life complete, calmed in the
strife and storm.

The weary worker without a rest has been taken from earth away,
But our dear leader will live again on the Resurrection Day.

Yonder's the hall wherein he sat and bowed his weary head;
'Tis strange to think—now he is passed—that his homely voice is fled.
Here is his Bible, with marks inside, that he used to read each night
While he prayed the Father up in Heav'n for strength and guiding light,
And for help throughout the coming day, for duties to be done;
Now our dear leader is gone away, his battle is fought and won.

On Landour hill he lies asleep under the grassy sod,
In the cemetery old, a peaceful spot, watched by Almighty God;
In memory's mirror his image dwells, and faith with steady eyes
Looks forward to another day, when above the starry skies,
In the land of love he will be seen in the joyful coming day;
For our dear leader, he is not dead—he's gone just over the way!

Arranged by his son, Norman E. Whipple, with apologies to Wm. Cuthbertson.

GLOSSARY

GLOSSARY

Ahir — a cowherd; man of the cowherd caste.

Anna — coin equivalent to four pice, or the sixteenth part of a rupee.

Baniya — shopkeeper.

Bhajan — native Hindi song.

Bhaktin — a Hindu holy woman.

Bhunjia, or bhujia — pot-fried vegetables with herbs and spices.

Chamar — caste which works in leather.

Chapati — thin cake of unleavened whole wheat bread.

Channa — kind of lentil known as gram.

Chota hazri, or better, chhoti hazri — "little breakfast" or early morning tea.

Chutiya, or choti — lock of hair left on the top of the head, and said by some Hindus to be the means by which a man is pulled across the river of death.

Chawkidar — watchman.

Dak — mail.

Dak bungalow — Government rest houses spaced a day's journey apart.

Dal — lentils.

Dandy, or dandi — a boat-like chair used in the hills and carried on the shoulders of four coolies.

Dawai, or dawa — medicine.

Deodar — type of evergreen tree which grows in the hills.

Dharamshala — rest house for pilgrims on pilgrimages.

Ghi — clarified butter.

Gili — wet or moist.

Gur — unrefined sugar.

Imangah — Place of Faith.

Jhundri — millet used for bread.

Kamise — long Indian shirt.

Kichuri — dish made of rice and lentils and cooked in ghi.

Kumbh mela — mela held at Allahabad every twelve years.

216

Kumbi — man of the farmer caste.

Lama — Tibetan priest.

Lapsi — sweet jam.

Lathi — long pointed staff used by villagers for protection.

Lota — small brass pot.

Lu — hot wind which blows in March, April and May in North India.

Mahua — Indian tree.

Magh — the month in the Hindu calendar which approximates January in our calendar.

Mela — religious gathering or fair.

Pagri — turban.

Pahari — hill people and their language.

Pan — leaf filled with betelnut and chewed.

Pasi — the swineherd caste.

Pice — coin of approximately one-half cent.

Puja — ceremony of worship and purification.

Sadhu — Indian religious man recognized by his white or saffron robes; an Indian ascetic.

Sahib — gentleman.

Sari — five or six yards of cloth worn by Indian women.

Sarpat — tall grass used in making mats and thatch.

Surahi — clay jug used for keeping water cool.

Zenana — women's quarters.

For copies of this book —
Inquire at your local bookstore
or order from:

**Rev. Tyrrell D. Fordham
5455 S. Catherine
La Grange, Ill. 60525**